FROM THE GHETTOS OF
PHILADELPHIA
TO THE SLUMS OF
KENYA

FROM THE GHETTOS OF
PHILADELPHIA
TO THE SLUMS OF
KENYA

BENJAMIN WILLIAMS PUBLISHING

WWW.BWPUBLISHING.COM

From The Ghettos of Philadelphia to The Slums of Kenya

ISBN 978-0-9909650-0-8

Printed in The United States of America

Benjamin Williams Publishing
18525 S. Torrence Ave. Suite D-3
Lansing, Illinois 60438
1-888-757-0007
www.bwpublishing.com

FROM THE GHETTOS OF
PHILADELPHIA
TO THE SLUMS OF
KENYA

This book is dedicated to:

Elect Lady Annie L. Harris
Elect Lady Idabel Sessoms
Minister Betty J. Harris

The three women this book is being dedicated to are the three people who were responsible for how I became the man that I am today. They have empowered me, motivated me, encouraged me, and supported me.

The Apostle Paul said I am what I am by the grace of God. That statement is the sentiments of my heart.But I also realized today that God used these three women to bring me to this point of my life.

Bishop J.E. Harris

CONTENTS

Chapters

Chapters

CHAPTER ONE

GROWING UP IN THE GHETTOS, BUT STILL HAPPY

We are going to start this book in a little town by the name of Norristown, which is 40 miles west of Philadelphia, Pennsylvania.

Imagine with me the sound of feet running and off in the distance you hear screams. Screams of men and women and even children screaming then the sound of running feet came to a stop. Then the young man fell down on his knees exhausted from running. He is a young African American in his mid 20's and he begins to look up as he is kneeling down and cried with a loud voice "Oh God help me, forgive me please,

1

please, please!" Then a shadow appears over the top of him. Something is hovering over him it has wings so large they sound like horses running. The young man gets back up and begins to run again. He runs to a small brick building and falls down. He looks up at the sign over the door and realizes that it's the church he grew up in. The whole front of the building had a rocky type of finish. He began to scream, "Hide me" and the rocks spoke back "there is no hiding place." The young man stood up and began running again. Eventually coming to a stop next to a dumpster where he sat down. He could still hear screaming from a distance. And suddenly he looked to his left and saw a tall man walking towards him. And as the man began to get closer he began to yell at him, "What's happening?" But the man answered him not. And then he realized this man had a uniform on. He was a policeman. He was walking like he was in a daze and he kept saying to himself, "I can't die, I can't die." The young man said, "What do you mean you can't die?" The policeman looked at him and said, "I put this gun in my mouth and pulled the trigger four times trying to kill myself but "I can't die." I can't die." And after the policeman walked by him he looked at the back of his head and most of the back of his head was gone. Terrified of what he just saw he began running again.

He came to an opening, which appeared to be a large parking lot with one or two cars in it, and suddenly he heard the noise of those creatures hovering over him. And then the noise just stopped as he began to turn and look around he was surrounded by them. He stood there terrified at what he was looking at, those creatures had faces like men with what appeared to be gold crowns on their heads, the hair was like that of a woman, teeth like lion's teeth and they had long tails like scorpions. He was too terrified to yell. They began to move closer and closer and closer. All of them at the same time began stinging him with their tails. He began to yell and scream like he never screamed in his life. Suddenly he rose up still screaming on the bed he was lying on in his cell. As he was sitting up in his bed still screaming you could see the shadows of the bars on the wall behind him. Outside of the cell down the end of the hall lights began to come on. You could hear those steel doors being opened and three prison guards came in and started running up the hallway because the screams sounded like somebody was being killed. Eight hours later a young preacher by the name of Harris left Philadelphia headed west on I 76 to visit the young inmate who had this horrible nightmare. Once he arrived he was greeted at the front desk at The Norristown Prison. He had visited this prison many times and one of the guards who was getting off duty said to him, "Rev Harris are you here to see that Johnson fellow again?" I answered, "Yes sir, his mother called me this morning." They had someone to take me back to talk with him and they allowed me to use the room used by attorneys and inmates. When he came into the waiting room I could not help but noticing that he was physically shaken by the nightmare. He said "Hello Rev Harris." I answered, "Praise the Lord Brother Johnson." This is the third time in six months you had the same dream. Then I told him, "Your mother called me this morning and asked if I could check on you, she told me that you said, "This time the dream was more real than ever before." Then I said to him "Brother Johnson, the Almighty wants you to give your life over to him. He said as he paced the floor, "I know. I know Rev Harris but it's easier said than done and you don't know what my life has been like on the outside and I'm sure you don't have any idea what it's like in here." I replied, "What makes you say that?" He said to me, "You just don't know we have two different life styles, I've been into stuff you just couldn't understand, not to mention what I go through in here. You just don't know, you just don't know." I replied, "Brother Johnson, you're looking at me for who I am today, right now, but I haven't been wearing a clergy collar all my life. I haven't been a preacher all my life, there is nothing new under the sun." "Sit down and stop pacing the floor," I told him. "Let me tell you where I came from. I have no plans for this afternoon and you certainly aren't going any place soon." I began to share with him some of my many testimonies, of what the Almighty has done for me.

We started our book long after our story began. As we get further into our book it will become apparent to you why we chose to do it like this. So let us go to the beginning of our story, in order to do this we need to go back to the year of 1944 May the 20th. It was a rainy night in west Philadelphia at a hospital by the name of Fredrick Douglas. A child by the name of James E. Harris was born to a single parent. James had two older brothers at the time of his birth, Joseph and Tyrone. They lived in a neighborhood that would be considered by many as a ghetto. I was in my late teens before I realized just how poor we were. My mother was a woman who knew how to manage by herself. Coming up as a child we were on welfare for as long as I could remember. I was one of those children whose father went out to get a paper and never came back. My two older brothers knew him briefly when they lived in Connecticut. I often tell people if I boarded an airplane or a train or even a public bus I might be sitting right next to him and would never know it. At the age of 67, I can remember as far back before I even started kindergarten. We lived on George Street between Nineteenth and Twentieth. At one end of my block was the back part of the post office. Two blocks up the street in the other direction was Corinthian Avenue. It was a big hospital there. I can recall the two toys I liked to play with most of the time. They were Walt Disney characters. One was Mickey Mouse and the other one was Pluto. They had moveable arms and legs carved out of wood and painted. Pluto was my favorite of the two. I remember how we never had a bathroom in the house until I became seven or eight years old. We had to go out into the yard to use the bathroom; it was just an outhouse in the corner of the yard. We also didn't have electricity. We used candles and kerosene lanterns. Yes this was in North Philadelphia in the early forties. It sounds like something taken place in the south but this was in the city. We didn't have hot water. There was a large room on the first floor that served as a kitchen as well as the dining room and in that room we had a big potbelly stove. It had six round metal plates that were removable for the purpose of putting wood and coal in it. The chimney from that potbelly stove ran up the wall and outside. My mother used that stove for cooking and also to heat up the house. We did have a large coal stove in the basement that had heat ducts going all through the house.

When we could afford to buy coal, there was a coal chute in the basement about once a month the coal man would show up in his truck and put his chute to the basement window. I used to run down to the basement and watch the coal as it came through the basement window. The coal stove that was in the basement had to be banked off every night so that you wouldn't have to start it in the morning. My mother had to cut up wood. We had a bin in the basement for coal and a bin for wood. She also had baskets of wood delivered once a month. But getting back to that potbelly stove up stairs. My mother used that potbelly stove for cooking, for boiling water, for washing clothes and for us to take a bath. Can you imagine getting up in the morning and having to wait for a stove to get hot enough to boil water to make oatmeal? Yes we were poor but we were happy. As I recall the amount of money my mother received from welfare each month was about one hundred dollars. The government also gave us surplus food once a month. One week you get a check the next week we took the letter that came with the check to pick up the food.

At that time they were giving out powdered milk, spam that came in large cans, corned beef that also came in cans, and cheese that came in a box. I ate a lot of cheese and mayonnaise sandwiches back then. George Street was so small that when a car came through they had to have two wheels on the pavement and two wheels in the street. We used to play marbles in the middle of the street. We would make a circle with chalk and put all of the marbles in the center and each player would have one marble and we would shoot at the marbles in the center taking turns and each time you knocked a marble out of the circle you could shoot again. As we got older we stopped shooting from the street on our knees and decided to get up on the pavement and shoot. Sometimes on our knees sometimes kneeling down and some kids were even good enough to stand up and shoot down at the marbles. Most of the young girls on that block played games like double dutch, hopscotch, and jacks. Down the street by the post office was another favorite spot. It was a telephone pole that we would climb up on and nail a basket to it. We would cut the bottom out of this fruit basket and play basketball. Basketball and marbles is mostly what the boys played on my block.

None of us ever imagined at that time that one of the kids who grew up with us would someday grow up and play professional basketball. That was Freddie Carter that played for the Philadelphia 76ers. He also played for about a year and a half with Julius Erving before he went back to teaching. But we don't want to get ahead of our story. I told you how my mother did all of her cooking, but I didn't explain how she kept things from spoiling. We had a back porch that was enclosed; some people call it an enclosed porch, but we always called it a shed. Whenever you went outside to the bathroom you had to go through the shed. In the far right side of the shed we had a large icebox. The ice would go into the very top and the things that my Mother wanted to keep cool would go in the bottom. My brothers would take me with them pulling a wagon seven or eight blocks to buy ice. We always had to cover the ice with an old potato sack to keep it from melting too fast as we brought it back home through the streets. Eventually they did start to remodel the houses on that block. We ended up with a bathroom inside of the house upstairs. They also had electricity coming into the house giving us electrical lights in the ceilings. They also ran a gas line into the house, which provided a furnace in the basement that had heat ducts running throughout the house eliminating that cold stove in the basement. These things didn't happen overnight but I'll never forget how excited we were when these things began to take place.

When I think about some of my favorite meals my mother made for us on that potbelly wooden stove, I sort of missed it for a while. One thing she gave us three of four times a month she would make a big frying pan of corn bread and sit it on the top edge of the stove to keep it warm and then with another frying pan she would take a slab of fatback and slice it real thin. She would fry the fatback and then set the table before us and pour karo syrup into the plate. Then after that she would take a little bit of the hot grease and pour it in the center of the plate on the syrup and giving us two or three slices of fatback and used the corn bread to soak up the syrup. Yes, we were poor but we were happy. There was a place three blocks from our house on Ridge Ave that used to give us chicken backs and chittlins. For a long time they gave this away free until they realized that so many people in and around our neighborhood was eating fried chicken backs and taking hog maws and chittlins and eating it like it was a delicacy. Then they stopped giving it away and began to sell it. I never realized how close the rich people lived until I started school. Remember I told you two blocks up the street was Corinthian Ave. At George and Corinthian there was a big hospital. Corinthian Ave was the neighborhood that the middle class and rich people lived. I had to walk through the rich neighborhood eight or nine blocks to reach my school. There was no such thing as a school bus to pick up kids at that time. There was some mornings our breakfast would consist of a slice of toast and a cup of hot tea. I can recall sometimes taking doughnuts off of the steps of the rich people on one block and go three or four more blocks and get a bottle of milk off another step. This was a common practice of the kids in my neighborhood. We knew that the milk man and the bread man would leave these things on a daily basis and my brothers and I would share a bottle of milk and doughnuts somewhere in an alley between home and school. No matter how cold it was in the wintertime we had to walk eight or nine blocks.

When I look back it seems like I always had holes in my shoes and whenever it rained we had to put cardboard in the bottom of our shoes. We eventually discovered that cutting the shoe tongue out of an old pair of shoes and putting it inside the shoe lasted a whole lot longer than cardboard. As a child I remember trying to earn money to help the family's income. I had a paper route that I did before I went to school. But it wasn't the kind of paper route where you deliver newspapers to homes. It was just the opposite. I would get up an hour and a half earlier than most kids would normally get up and go through the neighborhood on trash day collecting newspapers. When I had a wagon full of papers I would take them back home and store them in the shed for 5 or 6 days. Then at the end of a week my brothers and I would make two or three trips to the salvaging place that paid for scrap metal and papers. We would earn about four dollars a month. It wasn't a lot at that time but it was help. Maybe twice a month my mother would allow us to go to the movies on Ridge Ave and she would give us twenty-six cents apiece. It was thirteen cents to get in so that would leave us thirteen cents apiece. We couldn't afford the popcorn and candies that the movies sold but with thirteen cents we could buy a dozen of doughnuts at the stale Bakery on Ridge Ave. So we would get three different types of doughnuts and sitting through the cartoons, the matinee chapters and two full length movies we would eat three dozen doughnuts between us. I can remember at Halloween time how none of the kids in my neighborhood would go door-to-door trick or treating. All the kids from Cambridge street, George street, Popular street, Hubert street, Opal street and all the other streets in that area would all go to Corinthian Ave and start their trick or treating in the rich neighborhood. As I recall it was about ten blocks and all of the houses were made alike on the outside. There must have been twenty steps leading up to the porch where the front doorbell was. Can you imagine going up and down one house to another trick or treating?

We never saw other white kids going from door to door. Whenever the doors would open the people were very friendly giving us plenty of candy and fruits. And in most of every house there was a Halloween costume party-taking place. Now that I think about it all of the white kids that we saw were inside of the houses enjoying the Halloween parties but we had a good time. I'm sure there must have been some white kids trick or treating somewhere but we never saw them in our neighborhood or in the neighborhood where we trick or treated at. Even the kids that lived in the neighborhood did not go trick or treating in our own neighborhood simply because there wasn't any treats to be given out that's why we all made our way to the rich white neighborhood. I believe we only had two white families in our entire neighborhood. There was a kid by the name of Porter; his father owned the drug store at 20th and Gerard Ave. There was another white family that owned the grocery store at 19th and Popular, his name was Mr. Rodgers. He had one son and two daughters.

He allowed most of the people in the neighborhood to run up a grocery tab and pay him at the first of the month. Very few people had meaningful jobs. We never saw his children unless we went in the store to buy something. They did all of their playing either in the yard or the store. Ricky Porter was allowed to play with us from time to time. He would play football or half ball with most of the kids in the neighborhood and around the fourth of July he was the only person selling fireworks. No one else had the money to go buy them and bring them back to the neighborhood. But Mr. Rodgers left his kids under lock and key. We had so many things coming up in the Ghettos to keep us happy. One of the homemade toys we built was a scooter. There were two ways to make a scooter. One scooter was made with two pieces of 2x4 nailed together and two parts of a skate nailed to the 2x4. The other type of scooter was made with two pieces of 2x4. It had two pieces of skate on the bottom and one 2x4 was nailed facing upward to the other 2x4 allowing you to ride standing straight up. We had a game that we played called half ball. Rightfully so because we would take a tennis ball and cut it in half. This was a popular game. I'm sure it was played in other neighborhoods and cities. We would take one half of the ball and float it to the person holding a broomstick. Just like in the game of baseball 3 strikes you're out. When we could not afford to buy a tennis ball we would take a regular garden hose and cut it up in four inch pieces and throw them and see if they could be hit. I remember the old lady by the name of Mrs. Woods. Mrs. Woods was like a block captain. When a family had a problem they would go to her. She used to always gather food from the Farmer's Market that was given to her and passed it out to anyone who needed some extra food. Whenever she gave us free hot dogs they were so old they were turning green in some places. But by the time my mother finished cooking them, sometime she'd chop them up and put them in potatoes. Sometimes she'd cut them up and put them in cabbage and sometimes she would just fry them. But when you started eating you forgot how old they were. I also recall as a child on hot summer nights. There was one light pole in the middle of our block and it was directly in front of Mrs. Wood's house. Four or five times each summer all of the kids on our block would assemble ourselves for the sole purpose of killing bats. I never realized why the bats reacted to that streetlight the way they did. But I can recall the kids having brooms, shovels, mops, and baseball bats. They would be standing at this light pole waiting for the kids under the light to bring down a bat. We had what we referred to as kill a bat night. Some of the older kids would just take dirt in their hands. I didn't understand it until I was much older why the bats flew constantly up and down the street under the light. There were large insects that flew around that streetlight. The kids that had the paper bags and dirt in their hands would throw it in the air right before the bat arrived hoping to bring the bat down. I think we must have killed in the course of a complete summer 2 or 3 bats a year. When the objects would hit the bat it would fall to the ground and everybody would pounce on it. Throwing bricks, hitting it with brooms, mops or anything else we could find and the next day Mother Woods would have us all come together and clean up the mess.

In our neighborhood we were like one big family. If a child did something he or she was not supposed to do the neighbor a block and a half away would scold them and sometimes give them a good butt whipping. Usually when you got home you got another butt whipping. I remember many times going across the street and breaking off a switch from a tree and bring it back to my mother. She would pull all of the leaves off of it. Have us strip to our underwear and begin to give us a whipping. There were several people that came from the neighborhood I came from that became successful in life.

I lived in the projects for a short time that Bill Cosby once lived in and we know he came up to be a great standup comedian as well as an actor. We lived on Brown Street between 19th and 20th not far from Francis Ville Playground. There was a young lady that lived not far from there named Patti LaBelle and she too went on to become a famous recording artist. We had some kids with some unbelievable nicknames. One fellow we called him June Bug. There was a young lady that we called Bo Bo. There was a fella named Bop. Freddy Carter gave me a nickname. He started calling me Hare. Like in The Hare and the Tortoise. When it came to running, nobody could keep up. I can also remember the first time that I heard my mother crying. She had received a letter from her youngest brother, I think in the 50's, I think he had been stationed in Germany during the War, and he was coming home to stay. He had talked about it in his letter, living in North Philadelphia. And, naturally, she was so excited to know that her brother, who God had blessed to make it home safely was going to live in the same city, as opposed to moving back down south. Well, as it turned out, he had sent her to find an apartment for him and his bride. He married a Caucasian lady in Germany. We used to watch "I love Lucy," coming up as children. And this lady reminded me of Lucille Ball because she was Caucasian, tall and had red hair. I never knew that Black people could marry other people other than their own race. Well a few months went by and my uncle showed up with his new bride. My mother was extremely happy to see them. Some of the neighbors were there when they came, and surprisingly enough, nobody treated her any differently. The only white people I'd ever seen in our neighborhood were the ones that ran the stores. Well, it came time to go and see the apartment. My brothers and I went with my mother and a couple of the neighbors I think, and my uncle and his bride. When we got to the apartment building, it was my first time seeing it. It was up on the third floor. And she wasn't too happy about that. But what really upset my mother were the facts that after we had gotten into the Apartment, she noticed there were these roaches on the counter and roaches on the floor. It wasn't a whole lot of them, just a couple. You know, the normal amount that you see in any given day living in the ghettos. Personally, I felt like that was something that you just lived with. Being nine years old, I'd never seen a house that didn't have roaches. I'd never heard of an exterminator until I became grown. But she really acted out and started yelling at her husband. I can't live here; no way I can stay here with these bugs. That really crushed my mother to the point where she actually broke down and cried. Now I was too young to really understand what was really happening, but I knew that this woman had said something that truly hurt my mother's feelings. And I knew at that point, I didn't think I was gonna like her at all. I really wanted to mention this because I found that some 58 years after this had taken place that I was going to be guilty of the same thing because of something that I'd almost done myself some 58 years later.

CHAPTER TWO

A TEENAGER IN THE GHETTOS

I don't think I need to spend any more time talking about my early childhood days. So at this time we are going to move forward and deal with my time in the ghetto of Philadelphia as a teenager. When I was about thirteen years old I worked at a hoagie shop on Nineteenth Street. There was an Italian fellow by the name Mike. Mike was a middle aged, heavy set, tall Italian. He made the best Hoagies in Philadelphia. Nobody made a hoagie like Mike could make one. My main job was sweeping, cleaning up upstairs, taking the empty soda bottles down and bringing up full bottles, as they were needed.

There was this young black lady that worked for Mike and she always referred to me as a young black James Dean. I believe that the way I wore my hair at the time had a lot to do with it. Back then old folks as well as the young folks had this white stuff that we would put on our heads and it would straighten it. It would burn your hair. After you would get it to where you want it you put finger waves in it. I had a large curl in the top of my head sort of like how Clark Gabel wore his hair. Elvis Presley had one; it was a large curl that hung down off the top of your forehead. James Dean wore his hair like that. I guess maybe I resembled him or he resembled me. But she always laughed when she saw me and called me a young black James Dean. If you don't remember him, he was the fellow who made the classic movie called Giant. I believe it was the last film he made. He died in an automobile accident.

Now, Mike was a real nice fellow. He didn't live in our neighborhood. I believe I told you we had two white families that actually lived in the neighborhood. Mr. Rogers who had the grocery store and there was Mr. Porter who had the drug store. We also had a fellow by the name of Johnny. Johnny was a prominent young black man in his middle or late twenties. He was a businessman and he ended up committing suicide. He had several businesses. He had a seafood restaurant between two of the most popular bars on Ridge Avenue and one block away from that he had a mechanic shop. Half of a block from there he ended up buying Mike's hoagie shop, which became Johnny Lee's Place. He also had a body and fender shop. A very prominent young black man who was highly respected and we don't till this day know why he took his own life. He had a nice family and a nice wife. But he eventually took his life. He shot himself.

I never really gave my mother any problems or got into

trouble until I became a teenager. I remember running into this fellow who lived on Opal Street. He was much older than I was at that time. He was about sixteen or seventeen, and I had just turned thirteen. He asked me to come over his house to show me something. So we got there and I spoke to his mother. We went up to his room and he took this large bag out. I don't recall or remember if it was a cloth bag or paper bag but it was a bag and he dumped it out on his bed. It was a big pile of change; nickels, dimes and quarters. He went on to tell me that I could make money like this also if I was to help him. He almost got caught breaking into parking meters and he needed somebody to look out for him while he breaks into parking meters. Well, I went out a couple times and I looked out for him. Let him know if it was a policeman coming or whatever. They had a lot of foot patrolmen at the time up and down Ridge Avenue and Gerard Avenue. I was his lookout. Eventually I decided to break in my own parking meters. So I recall this one night, I was out there with my screwdriver and hammer breaking into these parking meters. Catching the money as it comes out. A policeman walked up on me and to make a long story short I ended up getting caught, went to juvenile court, spent a couple days in the place there in Fairmont Park for juveniles. They put me on probation. I don't think I got into any more trouble as a teenager but that was my first brush with the law. Breaking into parking meters.

Eventually I got a job at a service station. They don't have service stations today like they used to when I was coming up. When I was coming up you would pull up, somebody would pump your gas, clean your windows, check your oil and check all of your tires. That's when they had service stations. Today they just got places to pump gas. You can buy food and everything else. But they've gotten away from the service stations. I remember the name of the gas station was called Bob's Flying A service station. It had the big A with wings on it. You had to be at least fifty five to sixty years old to remember that type of a station. But it was a Flying a service station.

I pretty much worked my way up to doing a little bit of everything. I started of doing nothing but washing cars. We washed an awful lot of cars every day from Monday to Saturday, washing and drying them. There was a place a block and a half up the street by that big hospital on Corinthian's Avenue that I spoke of. As matter of fact the gas station was on Corinthian Avenue. There was an office building, it was an architect building and they had nice cars. The Volkswagen Bug had just come out. They had a lot of sports cars up there too. People from the hospital and from Gerard College also brought their cars to our station. I started off by basically cleaning up in the evening. There was lots of tires that had to be rolled out and rolled back in every day.

Sometimes, I helped bring stuff out before I went to school. When I got out of school I would go back and work in the afternoon washing or drying cars. There was a rag that I used to refer to as my favorite rag. I had this rag for drying cars and as well as washing. We had a fence that had this old fashioned wringer on it to wring out towels. Never realizing that years later that favorite towel that I referred to would become so important to me in my life today. But you'll have to wait till the book is almost over to understand what I'm talking about. But my job was washing the cars. Eventually, I learned how to fix tires even truck tires. We had a small trucking company that used to bring tires there and we'd fix them. I did some lubricating, oil changing, and simonizing. We called it simonizing when we used compound and wax. Sometimes you do two of them a day depending on the size of the car. Sometimes you didn't get but one a day done.

But eventually I ended up quitting school to help support

the household. I told you that my mother had been on welfare all of my life. I dropped out of school at seventeen. I ended up dropping out of school to become full-time at the gas station. I was still only making about twenty dollars a week at that time. Working from Monday to Saturday. I actually learned how to drive a car from working at this service station. I told you that I had to back them up to the wash area to clean the whitewalls better. Back then it was a big thing to have white wall tires.

I remember the first car that I ever purchased. I bought it from a professor who worked at Gerald Avenue and Corinthian Avenue. This professor had a 1948 Chrysler with a flat head engine. The front part of the car itself was longer than most cars today. It was what they called a fluid driver transmission. You can drive it as a standard shift or an automatic. If you wanted to switch you just push the gas pedal down till you hear it click. That was my first car. It was a four door. The biggest thing you ever wanted to look at. It was gray in color, all gray like a battleship. Matter of fact, that's the nickname we gave it, the gray battleship. As small as I was I could hardly see over the steering wheel. I had to get a pillow to put on the seat so I could sit on it to be able to see the hood, or to see over the steering wheel. That's how big this 1948 Chrysler car was and I paid twenty dollars for it. That's been some time ago.

I started full time at the age of seventeen. By the time I got to be nineteen years old the owner had enough faith in me to allow me to open up on Sundays by myself. There were many times that we had things that should have been done before Saturday at closing but it didn't get accomplished. Such as tires had to be fixed before Monday. Some people wanted their cars washed before they went to church on Sunday and we had agreed that if I come in on Sunday, whatever cars I washed, that money would be mine. But I also had to fix tires, do some lubricating, oil changes and whatever had to be done. The money I accumulated washing cars that particular day went straight into my pocket. What I would do is get there seven o'clock and people would leave extra keys at the station and I would pick their cars up. Most of them lived within a block and a half but, sometimes as far away as two blocks. But I would go and pick up their cars and bring them back to the station. I would do four or five cars by the time they wanted to leave out for church. So this is what I did from the time I was seventeen and a half till about the time I finally left this particular job and found something much better.   At the age of eighteen and working seven days a week I didn't have much of a social life at all. My social life consisted of hanging around the local speakeasy. We called it a speakeasy because it was a place you could go and buy liquor, whisky and beer or whatever you wanted to drink. At the time it was illegal to sell alcohol except out of a bar or state store. We didn't have a whole lot of TVs because it was a poor neighborhood. Sitting up in the speakeasy on Monday nights through maybe perhaps Friday. I didn't go every night but after dinner we would sit there and watch those oldie but goodies Like Peter Gun, Bonanza and the Untouchables. Yes! Those good ole shows. They don't have shows like that anymore. But that was pretty much my social life. Hanging around the Speakeasy I had a tab; meaning I could sit there and drink two or three beers and if I wanted to get a dinner. She also sold dinners. When I got paid, usually half of what I made on Sunday went to paying my liquor tab that I had ran up during the week.

CHAPTER THREE

Two Failed Robbery Attempts

I **had a couple of cousins** and sometimes I would hang out with them. We would go cruising. Meaning we would get in a car and we would go to places like Pat's Steakhouse on 33rd Street across From the park. You hear a lot about South Philly Steaks but I don't believe anybody made cheese steaks like Pat's in North Philadelphia. Back then we could buy two dollars-worth of gas and drive all night. Gas was about twenty-eight cents a gallon. Now I had been working seven days a week, from the age of eighteen to about twenty. My three cousins and a good friend named Leroy, and I want you to remember the name Leroy because Leroy and that rag I talked about being my favorite rag had an effect on my life sometime in the future. We would all go to the clubs on the weekends over in New Jersey. There is a place called Long Side New Jersey and it was nothing but clubs and barbecue places there. The Cotton Club was our favorite spot. We could go there and drink and listen to live jazz bands. Leroy was somewhat of a singer himself. He liked to mimic James Brown and different singers like Ray Charles. He sounded like Ray Charles. My cousins played instruments, one of them sang, one played the drums and the other one played the guitar. I don't know how it happened but I ended up being like a promoter or manager of this group. I would find them gigs in bars. I guess I had a gift for promoting things. I would get them gigs in different bars throughout Philadelphia. They would go there and play on Saturday nights, make some money and give me a piece of it. It wasn't all about getting rich, they just loved to sing and party. That's what we did. I gave up working seven days a week because as I said before, I had no social life whatsoever. Just hanging out in a speakeasy. All of my money was mostly going to the speakeasy. I would give my mom a little bit of it. Half of what I was making. Even back then when I was seventeen and eighteen I loved to dress. I would not go out on Saturday night without a tie and white shirt. I loved to dress in a hat. I loved that stingy brim type of hat that I used to wear all the time. So, for the most part every Saturday night, once I gave up working Sundays, the five of us would get together and would go out and get a few cases of beer, a gallon of whisky, and some wine. We would just ring somebody doorbell that wasn't expecting company. Waking them up sometimes and saying, make some phone calls and get some people over here. We would just party from that night till the next morning. When I look back on it we all dressed up. We all had white shirts and ties. As young people say, we had it going on back then. At that point of my life I guess you could say I wasn't a bad teenager coming up. Neither was I a bad young adult. But everybody has skeletons in their closets. And there are some things we all wish we could take back. These are probably the two dumbest things I did in my life. Two armed robbery attempts. Dumbest isn't even the correct word. I would say stupid. I could have been killed each time. But if it had not been for the grace of God who I knew nothing about at that time, I could have been shot and killed. I could even be spending life in prison if somebody else would have gotten injured. But by the grace of God it never corresponded. Never happened.

One of my cousins came by the gas station one day and I don't even know why we even thought about things like this because like I said we all had jobs. He had a plan for me to assist him or help him to rob the company he worked for. Well, I used common sense back then at that particular time and flatly turned Him down. I told him I wanted nothing to do with it. Well eventually I recall sitting on the steps, I think we may have been smoking marijuana. That was something just coming out in our neighborhood. We was just sitting there chilling, smoking marijuana. Somebody came up with the idea to rob a candy store. A mom and pop candy store across town. We went over across town to this little candy store on a little small narrow street. Hardly anybody was in sight. I think it was an old man. A Polish man behind the counter. We went in. Put these hoods over our faces and I don't even know who was holding the gun at that time or the starter pistol. We started demanding the money out of the cash register. Well this little old lady came out from back of the store. There were curtains hanging up. She opened the curtains up. She saw what was going on and began to scream and yell, "Please, please we don't have no money!" She put her hands up on her cheek, up on her face and started asking us to please leave because they were poor people. They didn't have any money. I kind of felt bad for the lady I went into my pocket, I think I might have had about six dollars. Which was a lot of money at the time. I went into my pocket and pulled out this money that I had and said "lady, please be quiet." And laid the money on the counter and told everybody let's get up out of here. So we left. Naturally they laughed about that for months. We go into a place to rob, and I ended up giving them all the money I had in my pocket. Not long after that incident, my oldest brother came up with an idea. Again stupid, stupid, stupid. I went along with the idea. I was going to call a taxicab to this dark street in north Philadelphia. One of us was going to get into the front. One was going to get in the back. But as it turned out, we both got in the back. Because passengers were not allowed in the front seat with the Driver. Shows you how much we knew. So we had the same blank starter pistol. My brother put the pistol to the back of his head and said, "Give me all of the money." Now let me remind you the fellow was sitting there with the motor running. I think he must have still had the car in drive. He slams on the gas pedal. He's going up the street blowing the horn at about fifty miles per hour. My brother is telling me to jump, jump, jump and I'm telling him no, you jump. Eventually the driver hits this intersection and slams on the brakes. We immediately, as a matter of fact, just before the car came to a complete stop, we both jumped out and ran. Again it was a dumb, stupid experience. One that I would always regret that I took part in.

I remember things began to slow down in our lives. I was the youngest in the group. I was about nineteen or twenty at the time. We were all sitting on the step, on my cousins steps on Nineteenth Street. Leroy, the fellow that I told you about. He was the oldest; I think he was about thirty something maybe forty. And we're sitting there this summer afternoon on the steps. A car pulls up in front of my cousin's house and a young lady gets out of the car. The prettiest darkest young lady I ever seen in my life got out and yells over to Leroy. Hello Uncle Leroy, and went into his house to visit his mother and sister. Leroy lived with them across the street. I found out the young lady was his niece. So we began to talk, everybody wanted to know who she was and wanted to meet her. I didn't give it too much thought at that particular time. But little did I know then that we would end up courting and eventually getting married. Eventually I think we kind of became bored of doing the same thing over week in and week out. My oldest cousin eventually went into the Army, did his basic training came out and got married. My other two cousins began dating seriously. I think one of them got married a year later. But we kind of grew apart from the things we used to do as a group. Through my friend Larry, I met his niece. We began to date. I found myself doing the same things but with an older group. That is working and partying the whole weekend. She had a brother and sister in the projects at 22nd and Diamond Street. She had another sister that lived in south Philadelphia. I think it was somewhere near Fourth and Carpenter. We would get together in the projects or somewhere in South Philadelphia. Every weekend we would dance, party and drink from sundown to sunup. Sometimes we'd break the monopoly by going to what they used to call a cabaret party. A cabaret is when you can have people from other parts of the city. West Philly, South Philly, Germantown and North Philly people would come to one location buy a ticket or pay at the door to get in. You brought your own booze. You'd bring your own food. They provided the music and that's all you'd do. Drink and dance. All night long. We did this maybe once a month. But for the most part we used to party in South Philly or North Philly on Twenty Second and Diamond. The only form of entertainment we had back in that time that did not include drinking and dancing was going to rock and roll shows at the Uptown Theatre on Broad Street. People would come from all over South Philly, North Philly, and Delaware and all over to see these Rock and Roll groups perform live on stage. They had groups such as Smoky Robinson and the Miracles, Jackie Wilson, Temptations, James Brown, Gladys Knight and the Pips and many, many more.

CHAPTER FOUR

MARRIED WHEN I WAS A TEENAGER
OUR FOURTH SON DIES

Leroy's cousin and I started talking about getting married. My outlook on life and what I wanted for my family was based on how I had to grow up. Remember I said that we had been poor coming up in North Philadelphia ghettos, but we were happy. Well, I wanted better for my children. I wanted better for my family. I wanted them to be happy and well off. So, I knew I couldn't do it making twenty or thirty dollars a week working at a gas station. So I began looking for a much better job. I think I started to work for this company in 1965. Just before I got married. I was blessed to secure a really good driving job at a company called the Bud Company in North Philadelphia. I was able to move in one of the best neighborhoods in North Philly. In 1964 and 1965 it was mostly an all-white neighborhood. This neighborhood was called Tioga. Tioga was a very rich type of neighborhood. But again the Lord blessed me. Even though I knew nothing about him. Even though I wasn't serving him he blessed me. He said in his word that he would rain on the just as well as the unjust. But later in my life I came to realize when the scripture talks about being called from the foundation of the world sometimes he brings us different ways other than people brought up and raised in the church. So I moved into this nice neighborhood. In a first floor apartment with a nice balcony. That very few people used other than myself and my family. It had two bedrooms because we hadn't had any children yet. I was still employed at that gas station while engaged. So what I did, I knew I had about six or seven months before I was to be married. We had a fellow who had a charge account. He had a furniture store in South Philly. He also sold jewelry. He would purchase his gas a couple times a week from our gas station. I opened up an account while still working at the gas station. I put all my furniture in layaway. My wedding rings I bought for my wife to be, I also put in layaway. There was a man who was Caucasian. He was a supervisor at the Bud Company and told me to apply for a driver's job. He told me after the change over they were going to be hiring drivers. They had several plants in Philadelphia and my job was to haul steel from one plant to the other. So this is how I obtained all my furniture. From the first day we moved in we had new furniture. Like so many young people today I didn't have a God on my side. I didn't know him in the pardon of my sins. So I didn't know that I should be giving him the glory and the honor for the things taken place in my life. Everything that I had accomplished I looked at it as things that I had done.

Little did I know God had a plan for everything and a plan for my life long before I came into the world. Matter of fact from the foundation of the world he knew where I would be at this moment of my life. He also knew where he was taking me in the future. But it would take years for me to know Him.

I remember when my oldest son was born in the year of 1965; Stevie Wonder had a popular song at that time called "Merry Christmas to You." My wife was in the hospital at Christmas time. My oldest son was born on December 22nd. I can remember sitting at home drinking and having a pity party, feeling bad for myself. Playing that Stevie Wonder song "Merry Christmas to You," and in the words he said, "Will you be home before New Year's Eve?" Even then I really didn't know how blessed I was because I didn't know God like I do today. When I think about how many people that grew up with me in that poor ghetto with me are not here today. Many of them have died years ago, some are in jail and some are sick and up in age. God has truly, truly blessed me. As the songwriter once said, "Down through the years, God has been good to me." I had to be as old as I am now to realize how blessed I have been over the years. Our life style did not change because we were getting older and having more children. We still found time to go out and party as they say. But we just slowed down a little bit. Sometimes my wife would get her nieces to babysit and she and I would go to clubs in Long side by ourselves. We had bars we liked to go to in our neighborhood for four or five hours on Friday or Saturday night. We usually stayed till closing time. I didn't get into gambling until much later in my marriage. That was something that happened through the people I associated with on my job. As the family got larger naturally we wouldn't go out as much.

This job that I told you about that the Lord blessed me with, that I never gave him the credit for, it was a job that

29

made automobile parts as well as truck parts. They also had a railroad car division. They made Amtrak railroad cars and subway cars for Miami and Chicago. As we said earlier, I obtained that job right after they had a changeover. They make the changes in the automobiles and the plant has to close down for two or three months. Sometimes for six months or more depending on how big the change may be. I found myself doing various different jobs, even though I had a good income and insurance while laid off. They had Blue Cross and Blue Shield. I was in the UAW union, they would pay us subpay. Whatever I got from unemployment I would get a check from the Bud Company to subsidize my income. We were getting about 70% of our paycheck from being laid off. I didn't realize how blessed I was back then.

I remember how I got started into gambling. I was never much of a gambler. There was this long layoff; the company said that we would be off a year and a half or two. So what I did, my unemployment had run out and I obtained a job at a place called Heinz. They also built automobile parts and I had no time broken in the union because it was also UAW autoworkers union. I did driving for them. Also they had a plant up in Michigan and different other places like the Bud Company. Sometimes I would work inside the plant. I ended up in the press department; they called it the press shop. This was during the Vietnam War. They made rocket motors. I had a job also as an apprentice in the machine shop. Back then was when the assassination of Martin Luther King took place. I was working in the machine shop at that particular time. I remember working in this place. When I was in the washroom coming out, this heavy set Caucasian fellow came into the washroom laughing and he said to me "You know they got your boy today." I asked him "What do you mean?" And he said "They just killed Martin Luther King today." I can't put it in words how that made me feel. Not so much that someone had killed him but the fact that the fellow that told me was laughing when he said it! So it was a lot of things that took place back then that you just don't forget.

I was also employed at this company when one of my sons had died. Back then I didn't know what they called it but today, they refer to it as crib death. Even now I can remember what happened as if it was yesterday. I was leaving home one day early because this plant was within walking distance of my house. I'll never forget it, as soon as I turned the corner from my house I heard my wife's scream She called me "Jimmy, Jimmy, Jimmy!" And I knew within myself before I turned around to go back that something was terribly wrong. I turned and ran back around the corner and up the steps and by the time I got to the door it was open. She was sitting at the bottom of the steps with the baby in her arms. I took the baby from her and told her to call 911. I began to give the baby mouth-to-mouth resuscitation. They told us at the hospital after they had pronounced the baby dead on arrival that he had died from what they call crib death. It was something that did not discriminate, it happens in the richest and the poorest families. I didn't mention it before but up until the time my son had died I had given up drinking for more than a year and after his death I went back to drinking. Actually drinking more heavily and more often than I used to. As the kids began to get older and I began hanging out with people that gambled every weekend, my wife and I did not spend the quality time that we used to spend together. I found myself going to these different selling parties more often by myself. This added to us growing apart. In an effort to strengthen our relationship and our marriage we decided to buy a house in a different neighborhood.

.

CHAPTER FIVE

THE LORD BLESSED ME WITH A HOUSE LIKE THE RICH PEOPLE HAD AS A CHILD

Do you remember the neighborhood that I grew up in, in the poor ghettos in Philadelphia? Where just two blocks away they had the rich people's section where the houses were built up off the ground. They had ten to twelve steps going up to the front door. When the front door opens you could see all of those hard wood floors and a big living room and a big dining room. Beyond that a large kitchen, well that's the kind of house the Lord blessed me to obtain. I did not stop the way I was living. In the basement of this house there was a bar with draft beer hooked up in it. Almost immediately after moving in I began to fix up the basement to give it a bar atmosphere. I began to host Selling parties. We had all sorts of gambling taking place. I had someone upstairs running my card games and someone running the dice games downstairs. The section of Philadelphia that I was living in now was called Olney and if you know anything about Philadelphia. Back in the fifties and sixties Olney was the richest neighborhood in Philadelphia. Between Germantown and Olney sections you had to work in these neighborhoods to go into them. If you were caught in that neighborhood in the fifties or even the early sixties you better have had a letter showing you worked in that neighborhood. Black people would not go into Olney or Germantown for no other reason. So everybody wanted to come up and see this big house that I had. My friend Slim gave me the nickname of Big Jim not because I was big in stature or heavy or anything like that. Primarily, because of the lifestyle, I always went overboard when it came to having parties. I like to dress well and I like nice cars. I think the way I came up in that poor ghetto contributed to how I wanted to live.

Once I became old enough to take care of myself, I've always wanted the best apartment, the best furniture and the best colored television. I had to have the first and the best. When the first box type cell phone came out I had to have one. I guess that's why I was given the name of Big Jim. With the increase of my drinking problem accompanied with my gambling problems it seemed like it was never enough money in the house. There was times when I would give my wife the money to run the household and before the weekend was over after losing everything I had borrowing money, on top of that I would end up going back and asking for some of the house money back. It didn't matter to me if it was money for the mortgage or money for the food. That's how bad my gambling had taken over my life. I lost sight of things that was important to me and I was only concerned about things that I needed. I needed to gamble and I needed to drink all weekend. Let me tell you it's not enough being a provider. Being a good provider does not make you a good husband. Being a good provider does not make you a good father. I was losing my ability to provide and to be a good husband and father that I should have been. My drinking got out of control and at that point of my life I became a mess. I was no good for myself and nobody else at that point. When I look back on my life as a child in that poor neighborhood in Philadelphia and think about those steps I used to climb and those beautiful houses and be amazed at how nice the hard wood floors looked, how much space there was in the living room, and with that beautiful fireplace you could see all the way through into the kitchen and to think that God had blessed me as an adult to live in one of those types of houses. In addition to having unemployment coming in and receiving sub checks from the Bud Company when there was layoffs. But it seemed like the layoffs were more frequent and much longer. Because of my drinking habits and gambling I had to come up with some other kind of hustle to support my bad habits. So I began using my car as a "hack." A hack is like a gypsy cab. There are certain neighborhoods in North Philly, like 22nd and Diamond where the projects are. People that get checks once a month need taxicabs to go cash their checks and to go shopping. Simply because, no self-respecting cab driver wanted to come in those neighborhoods. The people in projects had to rely on these gypsy cabs, which Is more commonly known as "hacks." The checks come on different days of the month so there were always people getting checks that relied on hacks for transportation. Especially on the weekend. We had people who depended on the hacks to take them to clubs, parties and etc. Most fares were between five and ten dollars. Many times you have drug dealers that are traveling throughout the city whether it be German town, North Philly, West

Philly or South Philly. They also like to use hacks. 22nd and Diamond was the worst neighborhood. I would compare it to Cabrini Green in Chicago, Illinois. It was that type of neighborhood. I never had any fears or problems with being in that neighborhood.

If you recall when I first started dating. My wife had a sister and brother that lived in the projects and we did a lot of partying in those projects. I got to know a lot of people in the projects and around the projects so it wasn't a neighborhood I needed to be fearful of. They had a lot of characters out there, people that was hacking. They had an elderly gentleman by the name of "My Friend." They called him My Friend because that's what he would say when he would see you. He called everyone my friend. He was a person you would never see sober. But, yet he was out there driving people around day and night. We had another fellow by the name of Johnny Dollar. I believe this name Johnny Dollar is a name he gave himself. Every two or three months he would change his car. He knew a little bit about everything. We had a character by the name of Jesse. Jesse was a self-appointed ladies man. He would go hacking from Sunday to Friday afternoon and from Friday afternoon to all night Friday and all night Saturday he would be out there spending money on the ladies. Everybody referred to him as the "Dirty old Man" he lived to party on the weekend with the women. I came in contact with people that nearly cost me time in jail and one fellow I used to hang out with nearly cost me my life. There was one night in the middle of the week when I picked this couple up. They were supposed to be on their way to a party. The woman was holding a box that appeared to be gift-wrapped. But it had a phony lid that opened up. They asked me to take them to South Philly. Going south on Broad Street, the lady said she needed to pick up another gift at a store on South Broad Street. They both went into the store. Naturally I waited outside watching the door because I had not been paid yet. With that box that looked like a gift they started putting stuff inside of it. After about 20 minutes they came out. Little to my knowledge they had been shoplifting. So as you know you are responsible for whatever is inside our car. The authorities waited until they got back into my car and as I started to pull off the police car that was sitting behind us put his lights on for me to pull over. All I saw behind me was light from a couple of police cars. I went to jail right along with them. For about a year and a half I had to keep going back and forth to court. Eventually they threw it out the court because they would never show up. They were drug addicts and were probably dead or in jail for some other crime. Now there was three times that the Almighty spared my life. Back then I did not have the sense to know that it was God watching over me. One summer, within a few weeks God spared my life. Not once or twice, but three times.

I had met this fellow who was a dope dealer, about a year prior to those events that almost led to me losing my life. He was a big time dope dealer in North Philadelphia; his nickname was "Super Fly." A few years before I met him, they had a motion film out about this black dope dealer who drove a pink Cadillac and it had cow horns on the hood. A lot of people that was looking to buy drugs or looking to sell drugs would use hacks to go from point A to point B. This fellow was a well-known drug dealer. All of the hacks knew him. All of the hacks wanted to ride him because he paid well. You could see him coming from a block away. All the hacks would start putting their fingers up in the air trying to get him to come to their car. But he used to like riding with me, I think mainly because it was like an unwritten rule in hacking, the best way to make money is to get from point A to point B, and back to point A as soon as you can. In other words, most Hacks felt that you are not making any money if you had to take someone and wait on them for an hour or two. But, my philosophy was sometimes you can take one person and hang around that one person taking them where ever they wanted to go and make more money even if it meant hanging out for the whole night with them. Sometimes I would get a hundred dollars for waiting on him while he conducted his business in two or three bars. You can make on an average Friday night if you're out there all night Friday about a hundred and twenty-five dollars. So that's why I didn't mind hanging around him for three or four hours. Because I was making what I would have made being out all night. In addition to that all of my drinks were free. But, sometimes you find one or two people that will pay you a whole lot of money to hang out with them. I knew he was dealing drugs but as a driver I felt like I was doing nothing wrong. Sometimes you can make a couple hundred dollars for riding him around all night. So this is why he chose to use my car as a hack, because I never rushed him. If he's in a bar and wants to hang around collecting money all night. I sat there and hung around with him. That was right up my alley, drinking all night and getting paid. I wasn't into smoking crack Cocaine or using dope in anyway. From time to time I would smoke some joints with my friends. I really didn't know what I was getting myself into by being in the company of this dealer.

CHAPTER SIX

THREE ATTEMPTS ON MY LIFE IN THREE WEEKS

You know when there are drug wars people not only want to kill the people that are over a certain territory, but they want to get rid of everyone associated with them. It seemed I had this reputation of being his main driver. A lot of folks didn't understand that I was just his hack driving him all over Philadelphia. All they knew was, I was the guy spending most of the night with him. One could have imagined that I was a member of his crew or maybe even a bodyguard. So the first time I recall nearly losing my life, I was standing at 22nd and Diamond Street right in front of a bus stop. There was a self-operated newspaper box at that corner. One of those boxes that you put money in, then take your paper out of it. I was leaning up against a three-foot high cyclone fence. They had some homes that were one story high. That's the purpose of these fences being around them. While I stood there at 22nd and Diamond Street waiting for my next fare to come along, the city bus pulled up. Now one fellow got off the bus from the side door and he began to walk across the street with his back facing me. And I'm looking at him for some reason and he turns in the middle of the street and pointed a gun and begins to fire in my direction. I quickly ducked behind that paper stand after hearing at least two shots being fired. That was the first time someone attempted to kill me. I heard some people screaming, a woman who missed her bus was laying on the ground yelling. The fellow who did the shooting took off running down Diamond Street. A couple of weeks later across the street from where I was standing that particular night, there was a cleaners on the corner. The northeast corner of 22nd and Diamond and on Diamond Street around the corner from the cleaners there is a drug store. I was coming out of the drugstore right next to the cleaners. I saw this fellow jump off the steps holding with both hands what appeared to be a brown shopping bag aimed directly at me. Then I heard the blast from the shotgun. Seeing the bag explode in front of me. Now keep in mind I heard the shot. I witnessed the bag busting open. Now you don't have to be a genius to know that once the bag had exploded it would only mean that the gun had fired, and all those pellets were coming towards whatever they were aimed at. It was aimed at me. But somehow I literally dove back into the hallway of the drugstore. My point is and I'll never forget it. After seeing the bag explode from the shot gun blast and also hearing it go off. I should have never been able to jump out of the way without being hit. So this was the second time that the Almighty miraculously spared my life. The third time I was shot at and again this happened at the corner of 22nd and Diamond. The first time it was at night when a fellow fired a pistol. The second time it was in the daytime with a shotgun. This time I was sitting on the same side in front of the drugstore in my car. I had a two-door coupe with all of the windows down. The fellow was standing on the south side of Diamond Street facing directly at my car. When I turned and looked his way he was pointing a gun in my direction, and started shooting. I immediately laid across the seat and reached up pulling the gear shift into drive without looking up and hit the gas, sending my car racing across 22nd and Diamond. I went to a bar not far from where all this took place, maybe eight or nine blocks away. I needed to have a drink to settle my nerves. Once out of my car I looked at the whole side that he was shooting at. There was no evidence of anyone shooting at me. I came to the conclusion that whatever bullets came in my direction either missed the car completely or sailed straight through the windows of the car. Remember I had all my windows down. By me laying down whatever bullets came in my direction must have went straight through the car. So I went into the bar. You know they say if you want to know something or what's going on in the neighborhood just ask the bartender. It was a weeknight, not too many people were there and I got into a conversation after I downed the third or fourth drink that I had. Telling him what had occurred and how many times it has happened on the same corner. The bartender stopped doing what he was doing and looked at me in a way that suggested he understood what was going on. I should have also. He said to me that "You know there is a drug war going on?" And I answered him "Yes." He said the fellow you used to ride around two or three times a week is in the hospital recovering from being shot up. Then the bartender said to me "And everybody else that was associated with him has been killed or either left the state". Then he leaned forward and looked me again straight in the eyes and said "how many days a week have you been running with this guy"? And I said, "Two or three times a week". Then as we looked at each other it became very clear to me, there has been three attempts on my life in the past few weeks because people seem to think I was a part of his crew. Needless to say when I got up to leave that bar I never returned back to that neighborhood to do any hacking there or anywhere else. My hacking days were over. I pretty much stayed home and watched TV. Went to the neighborhood bar from time to time because I was still laid off.

As I recall I had two bars that was my favorite hangouts every other day. There was a place called Stella's Bar. Stella was an elderly lady, she knew that I worked at the Bud Company, but still receiving unemployment checks and I was able to run up a tab there. Pay her every two weeks whenever my unemployment checks would come in. She had a pool table in the back room. Sometimes, I'd shoot pool until they closed. I wasn't that bad at pool so that was another way at putting money in my pocket. We never played for a lot of money but you could come out with thirty or forty dollars ahead. The other place I loved to go is a place where I'd spend my weekends. This was back in the days of go-go dancers and psychedelic lights. I used to like hanging out in this place called "Up, Jump the Devil." It was owned by a fellow who used to be a narcotic policeman. I remember this one time I think it was on a Saturday night. I was in this bar and my wife walked in on me. I was talking to one of the young ladies there and the only good moral value that I had was that I wasn't a person that would cheat on his wife.

I guess the fact that I came up without a father had something to do with that. I didn't want to be a husband who went out and cheated on his mate. You know what they used to say, all talk and no action. Well, that was me and I just put on a big front when it came to talking to the women. But still on this particular night my wife just walked between the two of us and punched me right in the nose. I started bleeding from the nose so I went into the restroom to clean myself up. Stunned and embarrassed as I was I went back out and kept on drinking like nothing happened. Now my unemployment checks were about to run out, so I decided, well I think I better find me a job. I wasn't about to go back in North Philadelphia hacking anymore. So I began looking in the want ads for a job. They had a job for a tire repairman but it wasn't in the Philadelphia area. It was in a place called Norristown Pennsylvania, which was about 40 miles west of Philadelphia. To get there you would have to get on 76 west for about 30 minutes and you would run right into Norristown. Well, I went out there for the job. Remember I had some experience as a teenager and as a young man working at that gas station. So I knew how to fix tires that wasn't a problem, and I ended up getting the job.

My friend whose name was Pellum. He and I were laid off from the same job. So I hooked up with him and his brother and we went to one of our favorite bars in Tioga . You could buy a pitcher of beer for a buck. You could also buy cooked crabs by the bushel. So we sat there eating crabs and drinking pitchers of beer. Mind you we had been smoking weed before we got there and I started drinking something called "Top and Bottom." A top and bottom is a mixture of orange juice and Taylor's Port wine. If you know anything about orange juice and wine, they don't mix together. Sort of like how water and oil don't mix. That's why they call it top and bottom. So after about five pitchers of beer and ten top and bottoms, we decided to leave before closing time. I had to take these guys home because they weren't driving. But I decided since I only had this car for a few months, I was going to see how fast it would go. I got on the expressway and began running as fast as the car could go. I had already dropped Pellum off so it was just me and his brother Donald in the car. He started yelling, "Harris stop and let me out of the car!" But between all of the liquor I had to drink and all the weed that I was smoking I was determined to open it up as fast as it could go. I recall coming to a curve, needless to say I could not turn the car at that speed. So we went off the expressway and became airborne. Now the fellow who was yelling to stop, I remember he had jumped into the back seat before I came off the expressway. And that probably saved his life. When I woke up I was in the hospital, in what appeared to be the emergency room and they were putting stiches up over my eye. I remember seeing the police officer standing in the doorway. My friend that jumped in the back seat, they told me he was able to walk away from the accident. The next day, I found out the car was a total wreck. Again God spared my life.

There were many, many other times that I had totaled an automobile in an accident. In my lifetime I must have totaled at least a dozen cars. And this particular accident happened on the weekend so I only missed two maybe three days from work. I needed those days to recuperate. I was given a citation at the hospital and a court date. So because I didn't have a car anymore. I had to ride with a fellow who lived across town. A fellow by the name of Lee. Lee was an alcoholic to say the least. The man drank for breakfast, lunch and dinner. Somehow he was able to manage to keep the job that he had at this tire place. He would pick me up on his way to the expressway. Every morning, I will never forget it. Seems like every morning this light would catch us and this particular light would have us on a hill. We would be probably four-car length from the intersection every day. As I looked to my right from the passenger side of the car, waiting for this light to change, I always found myself looking at this little stone building. It was a small church. I believe it was on Green Street. Little did I know, that about two years later this little church would have a profound effect on my life. Lee and I would go to lunch at one o'clock on Saturday. This tire company was very busy on the weekends. So most every Saturday we'd leave for lunch at one o'clock. Because I didn't have a car he was my transportation. To and from work and we'd go out to lunch together. I'd grab me a sandwich while he went to the bar and get himself something to drink. We'd always had wine in the car. I can recall every now and then coming back from lunch we would be stopped at that light on DeKalb Street. We always seemed to be three or four cars in line from the intersection. I was able to look to my right of Green Street and I looked up the street at this little church and I noticed during the week you would not see anybody outside the church. But, on Saturday after we had lunch you could see people dressed all in white. Women with long white dresses and white headpieces on their head. I couldn't understand why everyone wore white. I really couldn't understand why they were going to church on Saturday.

CHAPTER SEVEN

Beginning To Notice That Little Church In Norristown

This was the first time I paid any attention to the church where everyone dressed in white. And it didn't take long to figure out that it was their lunch break because I was on my way back to work at that tire company after my lunch was over. But I never once thought for the life of me that one day I would be a part of that little church on Green Street. Keep in mind; I didn't live in that town. I lived in Philadelphia. Although my involvement with this church didn't happen for at least a year and a half later. It might have been even two years. We never know what God's plan is for us in our lifetime, even when we have no real knowledge of him. It is he that is controlling our lives. I recall hearing somebody playing the drums and you could hear someone playing a guitar as though they might have been practicing. But, whenever I saw those people outside of the church, the little girls all dressed in white, the little boys and teenagers dressed in all white as well as all of the adults. They really kind of amazed me. I worked at that tire shop for about eight and a half months. And every time on Saturday on my way back to work I looked forward to looking up the street and hearing that music. Eventually, I went back to work and it could not have been too soon. My life had taken a turn for the worse. I was drinking like an out of control alcoholic always getting on my wife's nerve as well as everyone else's nerve around me. I had developed a real, real bad drinking problem. I still never realized how blessed I was back then and at how good God was to me. My gambling did not end with my weekend losses. Being in a dingy basement shooting dice on a ping-pong table. Friday and Saturday nights. But, it also carried over into the weekdays. I can recall back then when I used to have to work inside the plant, installing windows, seats, battery boxes and wheels on subway cars meant for delivery in Chicago. We also made the metro liners that are in Illinois. We also made Amtrak's.

I can recall on our lunch break when everybody else was going to the cafeteria. I would be headed to the rest room. There was a group of us who would meet up in restroom and shoot dice on the floor yes; my life was spiraling out of control. When I lost what little money I had I always managed to go borrow money from the loan sharks, who loaned money at 25 cents on the dollar. By the time I got my paycheck, about a third went to my gambling debt. At this particular time I was taking home about 650 Dollars which was very good for someone to make back then. Providing they were someone that knew how to handle their money and wasn't gambling because in spite of my losses I still made what most people made back then. But when you think about the responsibilities I had it was a serious problem. We had four children at the time, mortgage payment, food, automobile and insurance with one person working, gambling is a serious problem. At this point of my life I had become out of control. I wasn't any good for myself or for anyone else for that matter. That little church up there in Norristown was completely out of my mind by now because I had not worked over there for little over a year. But little did I know God had a plan for my life for me to become a part of that church one day.

CHAPTER EIGHT

REALITY CHECK COMING HOME TO A BIG BEAUTIFUL EMPTY HOUSE

I recall coming home from work one hot summer day. When I went up the front steps and opened the door of the big living room, hardwood floors and fireplace. You could look right straight through the dining room that had a large chandelier hanging over the table and beyond that was the kitchen all new furniture because I was accustomed to having nothing but the best. How I was able to keep all of this with my drinking and gambling problems. Only God knows. But when I opened up the door on this particular day I found myself standing in a house that was completely empty. Everything had been taken out of it. I walked straight through to the kitchen. There was nothing left there but a small freezer. We used to buy half a cow and have it cut up into steaks and it would last about a year. This was the only thing left that I could see downstairs. Before I went upstairs I knew that I had come to a point in my life, I was facing something that a lot of men had to deal with. A wife that had decided that she had enough. I had no idea at that time where she was or the children. We used to have a saying and I'm sure people still use it today. "You don't miss your water till your well runs dry." As I stood there in that big empty house, for the first time in my life I began to realize what should have been important to me. It wasn't having a good job. It wasn't having a big beautiful house full of fine furniture. Or a bar in the basement with draft beer. None of these things seemed important at this time. It should have been first and foremost being a good husband, being a good father to my children. Being a good provider does not make you a good husband. Being a good provider does not make you a good father. It's a part of your obligation and responsibility. I continued right on working. I didn't lose any time kept right on drinking. Matter of fact I think I started drinking more as well as using more reefer. If I can recall this went on for about six or seven months. I hardly ever did any cooking in the house; I usually ate out or brought something home that was already cooked.

I remember one day on the job while I was working a shop steward told me to report to the office. When I got to personnel I was told that it was mandatory for me to report to the dispensary. The company doctor wanted to talk to me. Personnel informed me that I would not be allowed back to work until the company doctor okayed it. So I went into the dispensary where the office of the company doctor was located. Not knowing what to expect. The company was aware of my drinking problem and they heard about the personal problems I was having outside of the company. As I recall I probably talked to someone on the job and it had gotten back to one of the shop stewards and they must have informed the company. Even this turned out to be a blessing because I worked for a company that had a union. Alcoholism is treated like a disease or sickness; on top of all the other problems I had they looked at my drinking as a sickness. After talking with him for about half hour, he recommended a doctor for me to go to. Because they do have a program for drug and alcohol abuse. It's in our contract which is UAW and that stands for United Auto Workers Union. This particular problem that I had qualified me for a medical leave of absence. They gave me a six-month leave of absence. My income wasn't as great as what I received from being laid off. If you recall not only do we get unemployment but we also receive sub checks and both of these equal about seventy percent of your pay. So even though I wasn't getting as much money it still was a blessing in that most jobs could have fired me. I believe I had to see this doctor twice a week in order to keep my checks coming in. He mostly checked my vitals and talked to me for maybe 15 to 20 minutes. Maybe every two or three weeks he would give me random drug tests. I guess to see where my state of mind was. But because of the good union we had, my drinking problem had to be treated as a sickness and it warranted my receiving a medical leave of absence. I would receive about 60 percent of my pay for about six months to a year. Which depended upon the monthly reports that the doctor would send in. So I didn't mind at all being off from work. The doctor that I started going to was in North Philadelphia. He was an African-American and I found out very quickly that he was a Christian. He was always telling me I should find a good church because people that suffer from the type of problems that I was having should have a good spiritual adviser and help as well as natural help. But of course I wasn't having any of that.

I still had a mind to do my own thing and try to work out my own problems. I remember my mother having a conversation with me about staying in that large house by myself and I really hated going there at night.

I remember many nights I had to drink myself to the point to be able to go to sleep.

Now she didn't have a house, she lived in an apartment and being concerned about me she suggested that I stay there until things got better. I made arrangements to give up the house; there was nothing to leave because there was nothing in it. I eventually did end up moving into her apartment and sleeping on the sofa. She lived in a three-story apartment building and she was on the third floor. It was around the corner from where I grew up at 20th and Cambridge Street. If you recall the house I was born in was 20th and George Street, one block away. The people that owned that building they lived on the second floor and they operated a speakeasy. Needless to say, that environment was no good for my mother or me. Before she moved from Connecticut she worked in a hospital up there so when she reached a certain age she was able to receive SSI. Unfortunately when her check showed up once a month because She too had a serious drinking problem, 1/3 of her check would go to her drinking tab and half of what was left would go to paying her rent so she had very little for herself. Being with her in that apartment did not help my problems either. I found that I had to have a drink in the morning to get started and I needed a drink to go to bed at night. When I think about it I was drinking from sun up to sun down. I wasn't drinking top shelf anymore. Even when I fell on hard times it was a drink called "Top and bottom" which consisted of orange juice and "Taylor's Port." Orange juice would not mix with wine that's where the name "Top and Bottom" came from. The orange juice would sit on the top and the wine is underneath it. But now I was starting to drink the cheapest wine on the market. They had a wine called "Thunderbird;" it sold for about a dollar a quart. Between the two of us we could drink 5 or 6 quarts a day. One night I went down to the bar at 19th and Popular. I also had a tab at a couple of the bars in the neighborhood. I went in to get a couple of quarts of Smit's Beer which really wasn't my favorite beer, but it too was rather cheap compared to what I used to drink before I fell on hard times. I used to drink Pat's Blue Ribbon or Budweiser. I knew everybody in that neighborhood because I was born and raised there. I bummed a couple cigarettes off of one of the guys sitting next to me then I went around to the other side and started talking to some people in a booth and bummed a couple more cigarettes. By this time I had bummed about 15 cigarettes going to different tables and nobody was the wiser. Then I got my two quarts of beer and treated myself also to a shot of liquor, which I also put on my tab

As I started back to the apartment, I decided to walk up George Street, which was the block I grew up on. If you recall at the east end of that block was the post office and there was a pole in front of the back part of the post office that we used to nail a basket to and play basketball as kids.

I thought about my childhood. I thought about the ones who ended up having successful lives that grew up in that neighborhood people like Freddie Carter who played for the 76ers who used to play with us in the very spot where I was standing, people like Bill Cosby who grew up in the projects not far from my childhood house. People like Patti Labelle who also grew up in the same neighborhood. There was a light on that street pole as I was looking up at the basket nailed to the pole I could see rain drops falling before I even felt them. Because of the way my life had spiraled out of control and because of where I am at this time I remember lowering my head towards the ground and I saw a cigarette lying on the ground. It wasn't lit but somebody had smoked about half of it. Now remember I had already bummed about 15 cigarettes from the bar I just left from but I still bent down to pick it up and immediately my mind flashed back 6 or 7 years ago when I was living high on the hog partying like there was no tomorrow.

I think I mentioned my favorite nightspot on Ringo Street, just above Alleghany Avenue in North Philadelphia. There is a saying that we use all the time, "What goes around, comes around." I remembered some seven (7) years earlier as I started into this club called "Up Jumped the Devil." A rainy night just like the night it was when I was standing there under this pole where I used to play basketball as a child, getting ready to bend down and pick up a discarded cigarette off the ground. I remembered thinking about the man some seven (7) years earlier who asked me, as I started to go into that bar dressed, plenty of money in my pocket, not a care in the world. He asked me for a cigarette and if I could help him to get something to eat. I looked at him with utter disgust, and I remember I didn't have time or wanted to be bothered with anybody bugging me for cigarettes or money. As I leaned up against that pole, I can recall tears running down my face. It wasn't the rain that was beginning to fall even harder. I began to shed tears because I knew that I had become that beggar. I had become that man who was down on his luck, standing outside bumming cigarettes.

CHAPTER NINE

HITTING ROCK BOTTOM AND WONDERING HOW DID I GET THERE

Usually, when a person has a near-death experience, they'll tell you that their life flashed before them. I couldn't understand why I started thinking about all of the things we used to do as a child on this block because I wasn't having a life-death experience. But I began to think about all of the things that we used to do. How we played marbles in the middle of the street, how we used to ride home-made scooters up and down this street, how we played basketball under this light that I'm standing under leaning on this pole, how we used to go swimming at Frances Ville Playground, how we played football up the street, how we used to kill bats under the light in the middle of the block. All the things that I thought about were things I'd done on this block as a child, and I guess, what I was trying to figure out was, as an adult, how did I come to this point of my life? I felt like I was at the lowest point, at the bottom and didn't know how to come out of it. I stood there in spite of how hard the rain began to come down. Actually felt like I was soaking wet. But I could not move. I felt like I had no place to go. I had nobody to talk to, nobody to understand what I was feeling inside. Eventually, I made my way back to the apartment. I went upstairs and sat on the sofa, right in front of the TV. As usual, I would sit there and watch the "Johnny Carson Show" with my beer and my Thunderbird. After Johnny Carson would go off, they had a show called "The Late, Late Show." In other words it was the last thing to come on any channel. I would usually watch old reruns until I'd fall asleep. It's been many mornings that I would wake up and find that I went to sleep with the TV still on. But that's what it was like during that period of time in my life. I was going no place.

About a week later, I remember going down Cambridge Street. I was headed to a bar that opens on Sunday on Ridge Avenue. When I got to the last house on the corner of Cambridge and 19th, I heard somebody call out to me, "Hey fella, where you going?" I turned around and looked back in the window. He was sitting in the first floor in a chair by the window. It turned out to be my wife's uncle, Leroy. You all remember Leroy, the fella who when I was in my young teenage years and up until the time I got married, we used to all hang out together. Well, even though he was her uncle, he hadn't seen her or me for a while. He just asked me, he said. "Have you seen the wife and kids?" "How's things going?" And I told him, "No, I still had not found out where they're at, but things are going pretty good, I guess." And his sister was called Aunt Liz, she yelled out the window, "Why don't you come and go with us to church on Saturday?" And I told both of them, "I just might do that, but I don't have the transportation." Brother Leroy said, "Well, you don't need transportation." Just hop in the Van when it comes. We have somebody pick us up every Saturday. There's plenty of room for one more." So I told them I just might take them up on it. I remember about a week or two later, coming back from a bar that was on Ridge Avenue, I went back past Leroy's house and he was sitting on the steps. He spoke to me, and I spoke back. And I said. "You got any cigarettes on you, Leroy?" And he said, "No, the Lord took that from me years ago. I don't smoke anymore." He began to witness to me.

Nobody ever told me anything about holiness or living holy. I recall when I lived up there on Ringo Street, from time to time; I might go to a Catholic church there on Leigh High Avenue. It would be like an early morning Mass. I'd listen to the man speak in Latin and leave church and go straight to the Supermarket there. You could buy beer at the supermarket, thinking I had salvation because I'd just left the church. But nobody ever told me about holiness.

He began to witness to me about how God had changed his life and how much better he's doing since God has come into his life and since he has given his life over to God. He spoke about the Holy Ghost, being baptized in Jesus' name. All of these things, coming up I never heard anybody talk about salvation the way he did or living and eating clean. It really stirred me up. I never had nobody explain scriptures the way he did. He had his bible right there on the steps with him. It was like the Lord had set me up for this, and I was taking it all in. I think the fact that this was a man that I used to drink and smoke weed with back in the day. Hearing him speak about salvation and hearing him quote scriptures from the bible made me sit up and take notice. It had an effect on me because of where it was coming from. I guess if it was coming from a person who I never knew, I might have rejected what I was hearing. But I was really, really enthused over how much the Bible and how much his salvation meant to him. That's what I was impressed by.

CHAPTER TEN

MY FIRST VISIT TO MOTHER SESSOMS CHURCH IN NORRISTOWN

Not long after I had agreed to go to church one Saturday morning and I even got dressed up with a suit and tie. It wasn't all white. Everybody up there in the summertime, as I mentioned earlier, they all dressed in white. The men wore white suits with light blue shirts, white ties, white shoes and white socks. White everything. I found a suit and I put on a tie and sure enough, I went there that Saturday morning. We waited for the ride to come pick us up. There was this young preacher who had a couple of kids at that time, I think three (3) or four (4) kids and his wife came in this motor home to pick us up.

That next week, I had gotten a telegram from my company that I was employed with, telling me that the doctor had released me to come back to work and that I was to report back to work in 10 days. Well, it couldn't have come any sooner. I had gone to church with Brother Leroy and his sister, maybe two or three times. Then I started back to work. I didn't give up drinking or smoking but I found that I had slowed down tremendously. I never told Brother Leroy or anybody else for that matter, that, the church they invited me to and I attended two or three times before returning back to work, it was the same little church that I used to look at on my lunch break and sometimes in the morning up there in Norristown.

Now, remember the first time that I started noticing this little church in Norristown, my wife and I was together. Little did I know back then that God had a plan for my life, and I was still at my mother's Apartment. One Sunday about a month after I went back to work, I was looking out of the third-floor Window, and I looked across the street, because remember, we lived on the corner house. I could see up Cambridge Street and the first house on the left was where the Carter family lived.

Remember I told you about the young boy who played basketball, who went on to play professional for the Philadelphia 76ers. His parents still lived or his mother still lived in that house. I noticed his sister was sitting on the steps. So I just decided, I had not seen her in a long time, just to go down and talk to her. I wasn't doing anything. It was Sunday, and as I said I wasn't drinking like I used to. I was more or less drinking socially. So I came downstairs and I started across the street there. As I approached the house, she was sitting there with her face in a book, reading. As I approached her, I said, "Hi, Alice, how are you doing?" She looked up and said, "Oh, Jimmy, how are you? How have you been doing?" She was sitting there reading the bible. So she asked me how I'd been, and I told her that I was staying across the street at my mother's house. My wife and I was separated, And she began to witness to me. She was telling me that God had saved her, and she just believed him for her husband and their marriage. So as you can see, we both had something in common. Before I left, she told me that she had gotten an invitation to a church up in Germantown for next Saturday and asked me if I would like to go. I mentioned to her that I had been going to a church myself on Saturday up in Norristown. Little did I know that the place she invited me to go used to be part of the same organization as the people up there in Norristown. So that next Saturday, I went over and picked her up. We went up to a church in Germantown Pennsylvania and the Pastor's name was Lady Daley. I'll never forget the message that she preached. Her subject was "Haircut in the Wrong Barbershop." She preached about Samson and Delilah and there were some men there that, little did I know would someday become good friends of mine. People that I admire and look up to. There was an elder by the name of Berno, and there was another Elder by the name of Frasier. These two men eventually would be Bishops in the House of God, the organization that I would someday become a part of.

I really enjoyed myself being with Alice. After we left the church, I took her to dinner. I believe we went to Denny's Restaurant. It was at this Denny's that she introduced me to hot apple pie with a scoop of ice cream on the top of it. I started hanging out with Alice two maybe three times a week in the evening after work. I really began to look forward to getting off from work. She was a young woman who was going to church an awful lot. I believe her Mother's church was a few blocks down the street at 20th and Parish. They had bible class one night through the week. They were always having different speakers come in. She also belonged to a prayer band.

What this consists of was a group of people that would get together at different houses every Wednesday I think, at 7:00. They would go there, share testimonies and have prayer. Afterwards, they would have snacks and then go home. I didn't realize it, but God was beginning to really deal with me. I didn't realize how much I was taking that type of lifestyle in. I had stopped gambling completely. I still had not given up drinking or smoking entirely because it was something that I had did all my life. I stopped using marijuana but from time to time, I would get me a quart of beer or stop and get something to drink at a bar. But the difference was, I wasn't watching the Late, Late Show until time for me to go to sleep. I was getting up much earlier because I was working, but I spent a lot of time at the kitchen table, reading the bible. I started looking forward to getting off from work and spending time with Alice. Now, understand the relationship that we had was not one of a boyfriend/girlfriend type of relationship. That wasn't what I was looking for, and it certainly wasn't what she was looking for. Every time she spoke about her marriage, she was giving God the glory and believing the Almighty for her husband's salvation. We had a lot in common in that respect. She was helping me to deal with the empty void in my life. She always had a testimony that if I gave God the time, he would do the work.

I remember one Wednesday evening on our way back from the prayer band meeting. She suggested to me that I should start going back to that church up there in Norristown. I had not been in awhile. So I invited her to go with me, and she said, "Okay, I'll go with you this Saturday, if you like. So that Saturday morning, I picked her up, and we headed out to Norristown, Pennsylvania. Now, Norristown is a small town, and I found that most of the people lived within walking distance of the church. After getting about a block and a half from the church, it seemed like no matter which direction you looked in, you saw people that were going to the church. I could tell they were headed to the same place that I was going because they were all dressed in white. This was on Saturday morning. People don't dress up in white suits and white dresses going to a yard sale or a supermarket. So I knew that they were all going to the same church that I was headed to.

The pastor there was an elderly woman by the name of Ida Bell Sessoms. This was the first time in my life I come to realize that women could pastor a church. Over the years I've never heard of a woman pastoring a church. I've attended a lot of Baptist churches, coming up, and as I said before, I was separated from my wife. I used to attend a catholic church, but I'd never, ever heard of a woman being the pastor over a church. It was as strange to me as hearing about holiness, hearing about the Baptism of the Holy Ghost. Nobody ever spoke to me about speaking in tongues once you receive the Baptism of the Holy Ghost. So all of this was kind of new to me. But I knew that, and felt that God was working things out in my life. I was just going with the flow and enjoying it

CHAPTER ELEVEN

REMEMBERING BEING BAPTIZED WHEN I WAS A CHILD

Mother Sessoms had an assistant pastor who was a young man in his middle 20s, about 25.

And I used to go quite regularly on Saturdays and sometimes on Friday nights. This young man used to teach and preach a great deal and every opportunity on the sanctification of baptism. In other words, what is supposed to happen? What is supposed to take place when you go down in that water? Something supernatural should take place. And I've never had anybody teach or preach to me on that particular subject of baptism the way this man did. He came out of the sixth chapter of Romans. But let me tell you this first; I was baptized along with my brothers in Newberry, South Carolina. We were very, very young, 10, 12, and 13. My mother would send us down south when school is out every summer. She would put us on the train and send us down south to be with her father.

My grandfather was a deacon in a Baptist church. He had a nice farm where he raised turkeys and chickens. They baptized us in a river, a little small river. And on the other side of the river, they were shooting water moccasins. And I remember, even when I was a child being baptized, how the man would say, "I baptize you in the name of the Father," and before he could get finished, we would hear a shotgun go off. We would run out of the water, wait a few minutes and go back in. Then he will start over. "I baptize you in the name of the Father, the Son" and another shot would go off. We would run out of the water again. Eventually, the man did get around to baptizing us. He baptized in the name of the Father, the Son and the Holy Ghost. It was going to be many years later that I was going to realize that those were just titles and not the name; father is a title, son is a title, Holy Ghost is a title. But His name is Jesus. And just as important as that, I learned that something supernatural should also take place. And as I was saying, this young man, every opportunity that he had, would teach and preach from the sixth chapter of Romans, so much that I will get it in my spirit. It became a part of me. I told you how sometimes through the week, I would be sitting at the kitchen table, reading and studying the word of God.

And this was one of my favorite chapters. I used to love to hear him teach it. I used to go home and study it out, and run references. Everything he taught, I began to understand what he was saying about something should take place in that water. Otherwise, if you go down without being a candidate—

without understanding what is supposed to take place—you will go down a dry devil and come up a wet devil. But I thank God this young man taught and preached it until it became a part of me.

And my favorite verses were four and five. *And it read like this: "Therefore, we are buried with him by baptism into death, that like as Christ was risen up from the day it by the glory of the father, even so, we also should walk in newness of life."* Romans 6:4. Romans verse five says, *"For if we have been planted together in the likeness of his death, we shall be also in the likeness of his resurrection."* Now, what this was telling me, after being explained to me over and over and over again, that when you go down in that water, you go down in the likeness of his death. That water served as a watery type of grave. You should go down in the likeness of his death and come up in the newness of his resurrection—meaning that everything that is not like God is left in the water. That old man should be dead. The old man should die, and you come up in the newness of his resurrection. Glory Be to God!

So I wanted this. I wanted God to make that change in my life. It's more to receive salvation then just saying the sinner's prayer like so many people are doing today. They feel like repeating a sinner's prayer and saying, "Lord, come into my life and save me" is enough. No, something supernatural has to take place you have to also speak in tongues when the Holy Ghost comes upon you, like in Acts, the second chapter says, *"they spoke with other tongues, as the Spirit of God gave them utterance."*

And I didn't like who I was at that time. I didn't like the fact that I had no problem leaving the church Saturday night and going a half a block down the street and sitting in a blue and white bar, knowing that I just came out of the church. I didn't like the fact that they had lunch breaks, and after eating lunch, I would come upstairs, walk around the corner on DeKalb street some place and smoke my cigarettes so nobody would see me, then go back to church like I didn't do anything. I didn't like being a hypocrite. He also taught a lot about being hypocrites in the church and how that when God comes back, he's going to start his separation in the church because that's where the hypocrites are. And Lord knows I did not want to be a hypocrite. I didn't want to be going to church just to be lost.

So I knew I was struggling with things that was going to keep me from receiving the Holy Ghost. So the only thing I could do was rely on what this young man had put in me, and that is, believe what God put in Romans, the sixth chapter, that the things that I can't give up, if I fast and ask God to take these things, that he would do it. If I sincerely ask God to save me, sincerely sought him in prayer and fasting, to clean me up, to get me ready to receive that most precious gift, the most precious gift that any man, woman or child could receive. **But, you know,** in spite of how good I was feeling about how God was dealing with me and how good I was feeling about how God was opening up his word to me; how I had to repent of my sins, turn away from my wicked ways, the inner-me still got me to go out after leaving church and go down to that blue and white bar. Even parking the car, I knew I was doing something terribly wrong, walking into the bar, I knew I was doing something wrong. But I went in, sat down and ordered a beer and a shot anyhow. As I sat there, after paying for the alcoholic beverages that I just had placed in front of me I sat there looking at myself. I will never forget it as long as I live. There was a mirror behind all of those liquor bottles there in front of me, and I'm looking at myself. I could not pick up either one of those drinks, knowing what God was doing in my life, knowing that I had to spend eternity somewhere. And just like the time when I was leaning up against that pole, thinking about all the things that we did as children coming up, and how many times God has saved my

70

life, a tear began to run down my face. I was looking at some-one that I did not like at all. The person that I was looking at was myself. I got up, left out of the bar and went home feel-ing like I had betrayed the Lord, feeling like, as The Scripture says, I may not be quoting it verbatim, but there's a verse in the bible that says, we crucify him afresh. I remember saying to myself, "Lord, forgive me, Lord, forgive me." All the way from Norristown, back to Philadelphia, all I could say was, "Lord forgive me."

Now, the Feast of Tabernacles was coming in, I believe that is the week after the Sabbath Day, and they had a lady by the name of Evangelist Baxter from Cincinnati. Mother Sessoms would always get her to come and run the Feast of Tabernacles for her. The Feast of Tabernacles was new to me. This was the first time I've ever been in this type of service. It was through Minister Owens' teacher that I was beginning to learn something about the Feast Days also. They observed all of God's Holy Feast Days, as opposed to the days that so many in the world observe, such as Christmas and Easter. We only observe the Feast Days, The Feast of the Lord as it is said in the Book of Leviticus. David even said in Psalms, the 19th chapter, verse 8, he said, "The statues of the Lord are right, rejoicing the heart: the commandment of the Lord is pure en-lightening the eyes." Most people don't know what statues are, but if you run references, you find that when it talks about the statues of the Lord being right, it's referring to His Holy Feast days, those days that God wants us to observe in their season. Some people are keeping Pentecost, but they keep it whenever they feel like having a Pentecost service. I was so happy to see this woman and enjoy her preaching because I needed it at that time. I was at a point in my life that I wanted to be saved. I wanted to be baptized. I wanted to be delivered from all my sins. I knew that I had to go by the way of getting baptized in his name first. So we had a wonderful week, listening and enjoying the Word of God, coming from Evangelist Baxter from Cincinnati, Ohio. Matter of fact, it was in that service before she left, in that Revival I joined the House of God there on Green Street in Norristown. I had been coming for months, but I never actually joined and became a member of the House of God until Lady Baxter came and ran that Feast of Tabernacles. It was a most highly anointed week for me, going each night; well, I didn't make every night because it was some, thirty miles up to Norristown, but I made it as many nights as I could. I told Minister Owens, the Assistant Pastor at the end of the Feast of Tabernacles that the next Sabbath, that I wanted him to baptize me. I felt like I was a candidate. He always taught on being a candidate, how important it is to have a made-up mind. One thing I noticed about him when he baptized people, he always gave them space, time to get on their knees and consult the Lord and pray and ask God to do the work for them. This is something that nobody ever taught me; you must be a candidate. You must have a made-up mind before you go down in the water. With a mind for God, I'll live and for God I'll die. I was ready. I was ready before Lady Baxter came, and I sure enough was ready after I met her and listened to that woman preach.

So the assistant pastor told me, he said, "Harris, you go home and seek the Lord in fasting and praying, and we're going to baptize you next Sabbath day." Trust me, I could not wait till the next Sabbath came. I was going to work, smiling, going to work listening to gospel music. Even the things that I used to watch on TV, I had no desire to watch no more. I only wanted to look at things like the "700 Club" or wherever the name of Jesus was being lifted up. I was in the Word every day. Fasting and asking God to perform that miracle for me when I go down in that watery-type of grave.

CHAPTER TWELVE

I Knew In My Heart
I Was A Candidate For Baptism

So all of that week, leading up to the Sabbath, I pretty much stayed at home and did some fasting, praying, seeking the Lord for deliverance and expecting a miracle to take place that weekend. As I recall, when I was fasting, it's a whole lot different to fast when you can stay at home and sit around the house and do nothing. But it's a whole different story when you have to go inside of a factory like I did. I fasted a couple of days with nothing to eat or drink. But I was believing God for a miracle. I was believing God for deliverance. No matter how difficult those fasts might have been at that time, I wanted God to perform a miracle in my life. And he did not disappoint me.

I remember very clearly at the beginning of the Sabbath that Friday night, thinking about a verse, a parable in the bible in St John, the 5th Chapter, where it talks about the man who wanted to be healed, but he told the Lord every time he wants to get in the water, somebody would step in front of him. If you read that, you'll find, I think it's in the 4th verse, that a certain time of the year, the Angel of God would come and trouble the waters. This is what I prayed. When I began my fast, that the Lord would have an angel to trouble the waters before I step in it, that I might receive my deliverance. There were two or three things that I could not give up by myself. I knew that it was gonna have to be the Almighty to deliver me from these things. One was my drinking. The other was my smoking. Then there were the four-letter words that I used in all of my conversations. Although I could control my tongue when it came to swearing. But the drinking and the smoking of cigarettes I could not give up by myself. I need God to deliver me from these things. I knew that.

So on the day of the baptism, the daylight part of the Sabbath, Minister Owens gave us time. It was two or three others that were being baptized, to kneel down and seek the Lord in prayer for him to do the work. I don't remember what order that we went into the water. But I remember very clearly going down into that watery-type of grave, believing God for a miracle. He sure enough did not disappoint me.

Now, mind you, I did not come up speaking in tongues. Sometimes, you'll hear testimonies how people received the Holy Ghost while in the water. It did not happen with me that way. He cleaned me up for the gift of the Holy Ghost. When I came up out of that water, God had did exactly what I had asked Him the night before. He completely, totally took the desires of gambling, drinking alcohol; he took the taste of smoking out of my mouth, even down to the four-letter words that I used to use. That, in itself, was a testimony from the day that I was baptized, and I'm talking about some 40 years later. I have never used those four-letter words. And that in itself is a testimony. I have not drunk alcohol since that day. That is a testimony. I have not smoked since then. That is a testimony. But still I had not received the baptism of the Holy Ghost in that I did not speak in tongues, and I cannot stress how important it is for people to understand that speaking in tongues is the most important part of your testimony. If you don't speak in tongues, you have not received it, like the Bible says.

I can remember in the upcoming weeks and months after the baptism, becoming very active in the church. I didn't want to be just somebody coming and sitting in the pew through the service. I wanted something to do. I wanted to be participating in the ministry. The first job that I ever received was an usher in the House of God. I had desired to be closer to the church.

CHAPTER THIRTEEN

MOVED TO NORRISTOWN TO BE CLOSER TO THE CHURCH

So in about four, maybe five weeks, I moved out of my mother's apartment into the Pastor's house. She had a large house. I moved in and paid her room and board. It took me about 45 Minutes to get to work every morning and get back home, but it was no problem because, as I said, I felt a need to be close to the church. The things that I learned, living in Mother Sessoms' home for at least 12 or 13 months until I was able to get my own apartment was incredibly helpful to my spiritual growth. Mother Sessoms was the president of the Montgomery County Boarding Home Association. She had boarding houses throughout Norristown, four boarding homes in all. The mother of our local church, Mother Lyles ran three of those boarding homes. She took care of the business end. She hired a lady to live on the premise and this lady did all of the cooking and cleaning and fixing the brown paper bag lunches for those that had to leave out and would be gone all day. She would also be responsible for fixing dinner for everyone in that particular house.

Mother Lyles did all of the shopping for the groceries. She took care of all of the business end of the house such as shopping and the menu for the food for the dinner for that night. If there was any type of maintenance work that needed to be done, there were pastors who were carpenters and electricians, people like the late Bishop Perry. Bishop Perry was a man who was, I guess you could say, the Jack-of-all-Trades. He was very good in carpentry, painting, plumbing and electrical work. If he was too busy, then Sister Lewis would call Bishop Tate. Bishop Tate lived in Germantown. He was another well-known person who could do all types of maintenance work, cement, plastering, painting, electrical and plumbing. So Mother Sessoms had people that would take care of whatever the house needed within the church. She used me for much of her wallpapering and painting. Once she found out that I was very good at paper hanging and painting, I did a lot of that for her in those boarding houses that she had.

Where I stayed, there was a woman by the name of; I think her name was Ms. Cora. Ms. Cora was the one who did all of the shopping. She fixed all of the meals. She fixed all of the brown paper bag lunches. Every day before I went to work, I would have a brown paper bag with my name on it. What I truly enjoyed most about paying room and board at the Pastor's house was, by the time I got home from work, driving from Philadelphia back to Norristown, everybody else had eaten dinner. But mother Sessoms would always put off eating dinner until I got in. Ms. Cora would fix our dinner. I would sit there every day, eating dinner with the Pastor, taking in all of the wisdom that I could obtain. I learned more at that dinner table, listening to my Pastor in those 13 months than I could have learned going to a bible college for five (5) years. Around this time, I had also been blessed to have contact with my wife and my children. Even though I was paying room and board and driving a pretty good ways, I was able to give my wife some money every week for child support. We had not went to court for them to determine how much to give, but I gave her a sizable amount of money every week. She also allowed me to bring the kids to church from time to time. With that in mind, I began looking for my own apartment so that I could bring them up on the weekend and keep them up until Sunday.

The Lord eventually blessed me to find a nice apartment, three-bedroom apartment. It was just a half a block from my Pastor's house. My wife had agreed to allow me to pick the kids up. Sometimes I'd pick them up on Friday night and take them back Sunday afternoon. Sometimes I'd pick them up Saturday morning and take them back Sunday afternoon. Between working on my job and keeping myself busy in the church, I didn't have time to worry about whom my wife was with or what she was doing on the weekends. One of my favorite scriptures at that time was Matthews, 6th Chapter, verse 33 this is where Jesus said, "Seek ye first the Kingdom of God and all of his righteousness, and all of these things shall be added unto you."

There were many scriptures from the Word of God that encouraged me at that time when I needed to be encouraged. There was another favorite verse of mine in the bible, Romans 8 and 18 Says, "For I reckon that the sufferings of this present time is not worthy to be compared to the glory which shall be revealed in us." Then in that same chapter, up in the 28th verse, it says, "All things work together for the good to those that love the Lord." I really didn't have a social life back then. All I ever did was work and go to church. Work and go to church. But then again, when you look at it, I guess that was my social life. I also continued to be part of the prayer band. On Wednesday nights, as I said earlier, we would go to different houses for prayer. I also visited a lot of different churches, wherever there was a revival, wherever the name of the Lord Jesus was being lifted up. I had a zeal, a hunger to be saved. I could not get enough preaching. I could not get enough praising God in through the week. I was constantly looking for someplace to go and lift up the name of Jesus. I had a desire to be saved.

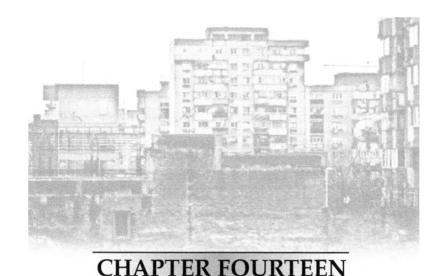

CHAPTER FOURTEEN

RECEIVE THE HOLY GHOST

On this one particular Wednesday night, I went to prayer up in, I think it was on Alleghany Avenue, right off of Taylor Street, and I really was not expecting anything different other than having a good time testifying, and then we all would go on our knees in prayer. But like the song that James Cleveland wrote many years ago, he said, "I went to a meeting one night and my heart wasn't right, but something got a hold of me." Well, to say the least, this is exactly how it happened with me. We had all testified. We all prayed. The way the prayer goes, it started off by one person. Then when that person finished praying, it just goes around in the circle. Eventually, we all end up praying and clapping our hands and calling out to God at the same time. Well, at this point, the anointing came into our presence. As I began to pray, clap my hands and just let myself go and let God be God. I had a made-up mind for God. I wanted to live and for God I wanted to die for God. I just wasn't expecting it that particular night. But God had his way in my life that night. So many times we think that we're gonna receive the Holy Ghost in a church, but God can come in anywhere he pleases. I don't remember everything that took place. But I do remember and I will never, ever forget it, as I began to pray, the words that I was trying to say would not come out. But I began to speak like they did in the Book of Acts, the 2nd Chapter, on the day of Pentecost. I began to speak in an unknown tongue. I knew what I was trying to say, but other words were coming out. The tears just starting to flow. Jeremiah said, "It's just like fire shut up in my bones." I wasn't disappointed in that either I became real warm all over. I would not stop. I had forgotten about everybody else in the house. It was just God and I. I just kept on praying, at least I thought I was. The more I spoke, the more I could hear the words. I knew what I wanted to say, but God was speaking through me. After I began to come down and come to myself, I could hear different ones around me clapping their hands, saying, "Thank you, Lord, thank you, Jesus." All I wanted to do was just continue to hold my hands up and tell the Lord, thank you, because I knew, without a shadow of a doubt what had taken place. I knew that salvation had come into my life. I knew that I had received the baptism of the Holy Ghost, speaking in tongues as the spirit of God gave utterance. I felt nothing but joy, joy, and joy. I remember when I got back on 76, headed back up to Norristown Pennsylvania; it took me about 35 to 40 minutes to get home. I was running real late. It must have been 12:30. Normally, I'm home by 12:00. But this was a special night. After the Holy Ghost fell, we had another testimony service. I knew I had to get up early. So I think it was about 12:00 o'clock when I got back on the expressway. I got home about 12:45, went upstairs and got on my knees, and I began to speak to the Lord again. I'll never forget it. I said, "Lord, I'm not doubting you, but if you've done what I think you've done, I want you to speak through me again." I began to pray and pray and pray. Then the tongues began to come out. I began to speak in tongues again on my knees, back in Norristown.

I made it to work the next day on time, with very little sleep because I didn't get in bed until about 1:30. I was up at 4:30. But I made it to work and back. In that day, we didn't have cell phones. I could not wait for the end of the day so that I could start telling people what had happened to me last night. There were a few people on the job that I was able to testify to them what had happened. These were people that we used to have bible classes in the lunchroom. Yes bible classes. The Lord took me from gambling, shooting dice in the bathroom, in a couple of years, to having bible class in the lunchroom.

So by the time I got off from work, the first place I headed was down in North Philly. Brother Leroy had worked at a place where they made dentures, and I knew he would be home by the time I would make it to North Philly. His sister would be there also. So that was the first place I went to. I had to go by and share that with them, although I would see them that Saturday in church. But when you experienced what I experienced you just have to tell everybody that you could think of.

They were excited and happy for me. My mother still lived up the street. I went up and I talked to her to let her know what had happened. Since I'd been going to church, since I'd been going regularly and spending time with her, sometimes

I would have one on one bible class with her. I became something like her champion. She really was pleased at the way God was bringing me along.

I called my Pastor from my mother's house, and she was extremely excited and happy for me. Now, by the time the Sabbath came around, everybody had heard about what happened to Brother Harris in Philadelphia. I was always on time for Sabbath School. As a matter of fact, sometimes I'd be getting there when Minister Rich or Minister Owens, the assistant pastor, would be opening the door. Everybody that came wanted to just throw their arms around me out of love and happiness for what God had did in my life.

That's one thing that I loved about that little church. We were like a family, a little church with a big heart. The Lord had blessed our Pastor to be surrounded by some of the best people, some of the best members you could ever ask to have in a church. There were people that I admired and looked up to, people like the late Deacon Albert Johnson and his wife, Evangelist Johnson, Mother Colson, the assistant pastor, Minister Owens and his wife Sister Benah Owens, a young lady who'd sing like there wasn't no tomorrow. She can play an organ just as good as anybody out there. I was at a church that had nothing but genuine love in it. So being in that type of an environment you can see why it's easy to grow spiritually. Then we had other churches in Norristown. There was the late Bishop Perry. He had a preacher's voice. He was what you might call a preacher's preacher. The man could sing and preach. Then we had Lady Washington over on Morris Street. We used to go over there sometimes for Joy Night. People like Mother Irene Butler. The woman was driving. I think she didn't stop driving until she was in her late 80's. It was Mother Butler and my pastor, Mother Ida Bell Sessoms Howard that eventually ordained me as a deacon.

CHAPTER FIFTEEN

ORDAINED A DEACON

Back in the day, Mother Sessoms and others had the authority through Bishop Rawlings to ordain people. Mother Butler and Mother Sessoms, my Pastor, laid hands on me in a state meeting. My pastor was the State Superintendent of Pennsylvania. She made it known that she wanted me to be on the Deacon's Board.

Around this time, the church was beginning to grow. The Almighty was blessing that little church on Green Street. We had a business meeting right after the Sabbath, and it was at this time I found out that the Pastor and the Trustee Board was looking at a property to purchase. It turned out, it was the Old library building, around the corner on DeKalb Street. Adjoining the library was two, three-story buildings that went with the property. The vision that my Pastor had was to purchase the library building, have the sanctuary upstairs and a large dining room downstairs. It had a commercial-type kitchen and bathrooms all over the place. It was the ideal property for growth. As I said, the Lord was adding to the church, even the apartment buildings. They had already figured out what kind of income these two apartment buildings would be bringing in.

One of the apartment buildings had a store on the first floor. So once it became clear that the trustee Board and the Pastor felt like it was the purchase that we should be making, we spent most of the time in that meeting discussing ways of making money for the settlement and down-payment of the property. If you can recall back, before I was married, I had a talent of closing deals, of getting work for my cousins that went throughout Philadelphia singing and playing in their band, something like a promoter. I was good closing deals and coming up with ideas. So I guess you might say I drew on that experience, and because I spent a great deal of my time going to different churches in Philadelphia, I met a lot of people. I came to know a lot of good preachers, good singing groups, and with my Pastor's permission, I put on a lot of different singing programs. We didn't believe in ticket affairs or raising money at the door. So I had to rely on people that would come for a free-will offering. We also used to have basketball games. I got involved with the junior high school there in Norristown Pennsylvania. I wanted to rent their gym. Even in that, I had to make some business decisions and carry them through; such as insurance for that particular night for everybody who was playing on the floor. I went out to King Prussia, and found an insurance company that would allow me to purchase a policy for one day for five or six hours. I paid for this policy out of my pocket. Out of the proceeds that came in, people would have to pay to watch the game. I paid for that policy, and still had enough money left over for the church to make a profit.

The way that I was able to get all of the churches in Pennsylvania involved was that I got together with all of the young men in Montgomery County. We had young men in Bishop Perry's church. We had young men in our local church. There were young men in Pastor Mabel Washington's church. So what I did, I got together with all of the teenagers and young men that wanted to play basketball. We challenged the churches in Philadelphia. You had Bishop Bermo, you had Bishop Frazier's church, you had Bishop Woodard's church. We challenged the churches in Philadelphia to play against the churches in Montgomery County. I think it was Brother Bermo, he's a pastor now. But at that time, he was a young deacon in his father's church. He was appointed to be over the coaching staff. He played also, but he pretty much got all of the young men and young teenagers, 17 years old and up that wanted to play basketball against the Norristown team. We also went out to Plymouth Meeting to the sports store there and purchased some white and black striped referee shirts. Oh, yes, we did it up big time. We had referees that we chose. We even had plays that we ran. We even went out and purchased a trophy. Now that I think about it, I think Bishop Peter Mapson in Orlando Florida who has the trophy. We also challenged churches from different states.

Bishop Peter Mapson at that time was in Lexington, Kentucky. We had an awful lot of fun getting together, seeing the Saints from different churches and raising money at the same time. But I think the best idea that the Almighty gave us was the dinners that we used to sell on my job there in North Philadelphia. I had volunteers like Deacon George James, his wife,

Minister Burda, there were some of the Hampton family that would volunteer. What I would do is I'd start on Monday. I'd go through the railcar department and the machine shop and take orders for lunches that would be delivered on Friday. We had about seven different departments. On Tuesday, I'd go to the press Shop and take orders. I would go throughout the entire plant.

Now, I would only take these orders only early in the morning before we actually started to work. At lunchtime, I'd spend 15 minutes of my lunch period walking around taking orders and on my 15-minute break period in the cafeteria. What they would do, they would pay me upfront, $5.00 for each dinner. Deacon George and some of the other saints, and Sister Burda, would bring the dinners up to the gate. They would set up a table, and they would pile up all of these chicken dinners. Some of the guys would come out, take the dinners and eat 'em in the parking lot. Some would take their dinners back into the plant. But every week, I think we must have sold close to a hundred dinners at $5.00 a dinner. So in the period of a few months, we made several thousand dollars.

CHAPTER SIXTEEN

APPOINTED TRUSTEE BOARD CHAIRMAN

My **pastor**, because of my efforts of raising money, she eventually appointed me the Trustee Board Chairman. Now about this time, my wife and I had been separated for about nine years, and I was still believing God to put our marriage back together again. I'll never forget, this is one of my testimonies, going to my Pastor's house and trying to convince her that it would be okay for me to work seven days a week. That would mean going in on Friday nights as well as Saturday so that I could obtain enough money for a down payment and closing on a house that I wanted to purchase, telling her that I wanted to have a house for my wife to come back to and see if this would be a legitimate reason For me to break the Sabbath. She told me, she said, "You know, Brother Harris, yes, you probably could make enough money to purchase a house, save enough for your down payment and settlement. But that would be you doing it and not God. God would not get the glory out of your life. I've watched you over the years, and you've always wanted to be a person that gave God the glory for everything that you do. So think about it, pray over it, but I'm not gonna tell you that it would be the right thing to do. God does not make excuses for us polluting his Sabbath."

So I wisely accepted her advice, took her advice, and elected not to work seven days a week to save money for the settlement and down payment. So after about six months of the company working seven days a week, there came another lay off, and all I was receiving was my sub-pay and unemployment. Out of that sub-pay and unemployment, I had to pay child support to my wife, which I had no problem with. I still was saving money, not as much as I would have liked to, but I was still saving money towards a house. To show you that little is much when God is in it, I believe because of the stand that I took to not work on the Sabbath Day, God just showed out.

I had found a house on Marshall Street, a beautiful house that sat upon a hill by itself. It was around the corner from the church, about a half a block actually from the front door of the church. It had four bedrooms, a nice backyard and a basement. It was really a beautiful house, and I began to ask God in prayer and fasting for that house. I even went around there one night and laid hands on the bricks and prayed and believed God for that house. Well, about four months later, the sale signs came down. The people moved into the house. Needless to say, I didn't feel very good about that because

I was believing God for this house. But, as I said, we don't know the mind of God. We don't know what God has for us. But one thing is sure, what God has for you, it is for you.

About six months after they moved in, the sale sign went back up on the house for some reason. I don't know why, but the people had to move out of the house. I went back to praying. Now, mind you, I had been laid off for nearly a year, still laid off, still don't have a job. Usually a bank won't talk to you unless you have a paycheck coming in every week. They don't just want you to have money saved up, but they need to see a paycheck.

The Lord had found favor in me, and he had allowed other people to find favor in me at the bank. I applied for a loan for that property. Within 30 days, they told me that they would be able to give me a mortgage even though I was laid off, with no idea of when I was going to return back to work. Although I had been on this job for about 14 years, they didn't know when I was gonna go back. They granted me a mortgage on that house. I moved into the house just before we had our National Convention at the church there on DeKalb Street. At that time, the National Convention used to move around from different states and different cities. It was being held in Norristown. I had fixed the house up real nicely. I had some people, the late Bishop Morrison stayed there and I had a couple of other pastors and ministers that stayed there. I had been called to the ministry that year. It was at this convention that I went before the Board of Credentials for the first time to receive my local minister's license.

CHAPTER SEVENTEEN

PASTOR UDELL FROM NEW YORK TALKS TO MY WIFE

We had a pastor by the name of Udell that came down from the Brooklyn New York area. She was a mighty woman of God, and she came to preach one Sabbath. I believe Mother Sessoms must have told her about the young man who had been believing in God for over 14 years to put his marriage back together. After the service was out, she made her way over to where I was sitting. Asked me if I would mind taking her down to speak to my wife where she was staying in North Philadelphia. I told her I would love for her to come and speak to my wife. The next day, Sunday morning the fellow who brought her from New York followed me down to North Philadelphia. My wife was living right off of Gerod Avenue. I didn't even call her to let her know we were coming. I remember ringing the bell and explaining to my wife who Pastor Udell was and that she would like to speak to her. My wife agreed to let us come in and we set on the sofa. Pastor Udell asked me to sit on one side and she sat in the middle. She began to speak to my wife, and talked for an hour. She had a word of prayer before she started talking to her. She told her things like the importance of having someone to love you and to want you and not only that but to do things for you. She talked about how I had gone out and found a nice home for her and the children. And here you are moving from apartment to apartment and what a blessing it is to have your own.

After about an hour my wife agreed that we would get back together and she was going to cancel the legal separation and move to Norristown. Fourteen years had passed I had been praying and asking God to bring us back together. Needless to tell you how happy this made me. I called my pastor once I got back to Norristown she was elated to know that we were back together and she and the kids would be a part of the church. Satan was not pleased he was not happy and he was not through. For a period of about 2 years she was at church with me every Saturday. She even found a good job up there in Norristown working for an insurance company. Her desires to go to Philadelphia had faded away for a while, but after two years she started to go back to Philadelphia to visit her sister. This was a place I knew quite well because I use to go there and party all weekend. She would go there from time to time. I never questioned her about where she was going or how long she would be. I bought her a car and she had a job at an insurance company. We had even taken trips to Lexington,

Kentucky and stayed in hotels over the weekend for our national conventions. So I really thought the marriage and our lifestyle was working. After 2 years out of the clear blue she told me in my office at the house, she said, "James I want to move, I want to go out and get an apartment." She found one right here in Norristown. She had made up her mind that she wanted nothing to do with the church and the lifestyle that I loved so much and was not about to give up. I think primarily because of the job she had and all three of the kids were in school that she wanted to stay in the Norristown area instead of moving back to North Philadelphia. So she found a place about 2 and half blocks from the church, just about 10 minutes walking distance from the house. I can't tell you how bad that made me feel. Sometimes I'd be riding up DeKalb Street and I would see my daughter jumping rope, just get a glimpse of her as I was riding by. We had brought her up to understand that women should not wear pants because what the bible says about women wearing nothing pertaining to a man. In the time that my daughter was coming up in the house she had no problem not putting pants on.

As soon as her mother moved out of the house and got her own apartment she just went back to doing the things she used to do. Doing the two years they were with me we didn't have a Christmas tree, but as soon as she moved out of the house they went back to keeping Christmas. It was very stressful on me to say the least. When you think that God has really done something you enjoy it and then to have it taken away for no reason at all, it was very hard. If that wasn't enough she decided that she wanted a divorce and that she wanted the house. So I spoke to a lawyer Mr. King in Norristown. This is the same lawyer that my pastor, Mother Sessoms had been using for years. He advised me to just give her the house and have her sign papers that he would put together that in my giving her the house she would not be able to ask for anything I obtained after the divorce. All of this took perhaps two or three months. At that time I felt like I could not live in that city any longer. I wasn't about to move out, give her the house and continue going to church around the corner where she was living.

If you recall before my wife moved to Norristown, I had went before the board at the national convention to get my minister's license. At that time Bishop Rowland was the overseer, he asked my pastor if I would go to Robbins, Illinois to pastor but Mother Sessoms told him that I had not been in the church that long and I didn't know much about the teachings and doctrine of the church. She recommended that Elder Rich be sent to Robbins, Illinois.

Now at this time there was a great movement all over the United States where millionaires were buying up companies for the sole purpose of breaking up unions. It all began back in the Reagan era. If you recall all of the airline traffic controllers were allowed to be fired and new ones were hired. This is when the movement to bust up unions began.

This particular movement was a little different than just busting up unions. These millionaires that were buying up companies and organizations throughout the United States, they did it to bust up the unions for the sole purpose of controlling the workers 401K and pensions. After they make an offer that they know the company workers are going to reject they make a fortune off of the pensions and 401Ks. Many people have lost pensions and 401Ks after years of service. But as I said they do it for the sole purpose of making money. When they approached us we were making subway cars for Chicago and Miami we also had an automotive department, their reason for having to close the plant down if we didn't accept the offer was that they could not compete with Japan.

They said that Japan could make a train at half the price of the United States. They gave us an ultimatum either we except a pay cut across the board or they are going to have to shut the plant down because they could not compete against Japan. There was a vote taken between the ranking file and we politely told them that we could not compete against Japan because we don't eat rice everyday. So it was decided that the company would fold up within 8 to 10 months. I had about 6 or 7 months with my seniority. So I had a lot on my plate at that time.

My wife had asked me about leaving the house and getting her own place. She told me it would be the following week that she would be moving out. So she had already found a place and laid away some furniture. She wanted to take the kids bedroom sets that were upstairs. She didn't ask for too much furniture, but she just wanted mainly to be able to leave quietly. And naturally, I wasn't going to argue with her about leaving if that's what she wanted to do. She had her mind made up. She had already paid for the first months rent and she asked me to help her to move with my pickup truck. I'll never forget what Deacon George told me. I remember asking deacon George James to help me move her up the street. That night when he showed up he said, "Let me see if I understand what you are saying. Your wife wants to move out after being here two years. She gave you a week's notice and she wants you to move all of her stuff to the new place." He said, "Minister Harris you are a better man than I am. I don't know if I would be able to do that." I just laughed with him and we continued moving the furniture. I never missed a beat. I continued doing the things I had been doing working hard, going to church every Friday and Saturday, in spite of how hurt I might have been and how disappointing things turned out for me. My lifestyle and my commitment to the Almighty didn't change. What really bothered me was the fact that my children were only 5 to 10 minute walking distance from the church; they weren't allowed to come anymore. They began to do all of the things that we taught against, such as observing Christmas and Easter; I don't think they went to any church at that time. But God was still good to us. I knew that once my job had phased out that I was not going to remain in that city. I found out through the union that if you lose your job due to foreign imports the government has a service where they will pay for you to relocate, and pay for training if you wanted to take up a trade. So I thought about that, I wasn't sure where I was going but I knew I was going someplace.

CHAPTER EIGHTEEN

MOTHER IS BAPTIZED AND RECEIVES DELIVERANCE

Also my mother was still living in Philadelphia, I was witnessing and having one-on-one bible classes with her. I was concerned about her and believing that God was going to do for her what he had done for me. If he had delivered me from drinking and smoking in the baptismal pool he could certainly deliver her. With that in mind I began talking to her about what she would do if I were to leave and move to another city or state. It was in that conversation, I asked her to come stay in the house with me. I was going to be there about 6 or

7 months and she could decide what she wanted to do. She agreed and decided she would leave the neighborhood where she lived most of her life. The Almighty was dealing with her she was still drinking and smoking but I knew that being in that environment would not be any good for her. She moved to Norristown about 2 months after my wife moved out. She started going to church and also decided to be baptized. This happened after 4 months of going to church, hearing the word of God, and asking questions. In my praying, fasting and asking God for direction as to what to do and how to do it, the Lord laid Elder Rich on my mind. This was the Elder that Mother Sessoms sent to Robbins, Illinois to pastor. I gave him a call and told him that I had about 5 or 6 more months before my job would be closing down, the government was giving me a grant to take up a trade and I was thinking about relocating. We had been friends for a while and we were like family. This was the same young man that would pick me up from Brother Leroy's house when I first started going to the church in Norristown. We talked for every bit of an hour and a half. I was convinced that, yes this was were I wanted to go and work with him in his ministry, and find a good trade school to attend, and I had been to Chicago once before. Lady Baxter from Cincinnati was the president for the missionary department at that time. She had hosted a missionary conference at the late Bishop A. W. Morison's church. If you recall she was the evangelist I came into the church under her ministry. She use to run the feast of Tabernacles for Mother Sessoms. I went out there for the weekend because it was her meeting and I wanted to support her. I loved to travel during that time when I lived by myself.

So I shared the conversation with my mother in regards to me moving to Chicago after the job closed down. I didn't know it at the time but once I got there I would go to school for heating, air-conditioning and refrigeration. She told me whatever I decided to do she would be willing to do it but she wanted to be baptized first. We spoke to the assistant pastor Elder Owens. We stilled owned the church on Green Street, even though we rented it out to a church that had service on Sundays, we had access to the baptism pool whenever we needed it. So he told me to let my mother know the following Sabbath he would baptize my mother. I was still having one on one bible class with her. I would teach from Romans 6th chapter a great deal. I wanted it to get into her spirit and I knew if she heard it constantly it would become apart of her. The scripture that talks about leaving everything that is not like God in the water and going down in the likeness of his death and coming up in the newness of his resurrection. I believe God. He has no respect of persons. What he had done for me I believed he would do the same for her. When it came time for her to be baptized again God did not disappoint us. She went down in Jesus name there on Green Street, in that little stone building and the Lord met her. When she came up she had no desire to drink. When she came up she was delivered from smoking. God had performed the same miracle in her life that he had performed in my life.

CHAPTER NINETEEN

AFTER TWELVE MONTHS IN A TRADE SCHOOL I RECEIVED MY DIPLOMA AND GOT A GOOD JOB

About two months after my mother was baptized I was laid off permanently. I began to get all my paperwork together so that I could take them to the unemployment office in Illinois. I also had this old mail truck that had the steering wheel on the right hand side. This was the vehicle that I was using to get to Illinois. I figured it would take about 15 hours driving 50 miles per hour. I decided to send my mother ahead on the plane. Elder Rich told us that it would be no problem for us to stay with him. He had a house with 4 bedrooms and had also fixed up his basement with living quarters. My mother and I both gave him room and board. This particular truck that I had, what should have taken 15 hours took me three days and three nights. Everything that could happen to a truck happened. I spent one night on the Pennsylvania turnpike at a truck stop, one night in Ohio and one night in Indiana. I had my toolbox with me and had to work on the truck every time it broke down. All of this took place around Passover time. I left after the first feast day and was able to get to Chicago before the end of Passover.

My first visit to the unemployment office I determined what it was I wanted to take up as a trade. It was a 12-month course at a school on the north side of Chicago called Corn American Institute. The government paid for my tuition. The school was on Fullerton Avenue on the northeast side of Chicago. I started school in the fall of the year. I spent the entire winter traveling to school. It was the coldest place I had ever been in my life. They don't just call it the windy city for nothing. I remember having to catch 2 buses and 3 trains to get there. Classes started at 9:00 and I had to get up at 4:00 in order to make it there on time. Many, many mornings I had to walk through a foot of snow to the bus stop. But you do what you have to do. I did not have a job the government was paying my tuition and my travel expenses were being reimbursed. There were a lot of cold mornings I had to get up and go to school. I still had children and a wife to support. Even though I had not been to court to determine how much support I needed to pay, every week my checks came in I would get a money order and send it to my wife every two weeks. I still had enough money to pay my tithes, support the church with my offerings and save for an apartment. Once I finished school, and got my diploma and applied for a job at Sears. I'll never forget that interview. I went to a place in Harvey on Halsted Street. They were very impressed that I had finished 12 months of training at Corn American Institute in heating, air conditioning and refrigeration. As far as they were concerned I had learned enough to start almost immediately and it came down to him telling me what their busiest time of the week was the weekend. They needed people to work on Saturday and Sunday. When I think of it the fellow told me that they wanted to put me in orientation for two days the next day and the following week I would get a new truck with all of the tools I needed to install air conditioners in the summertime and furnaces in the winter. He said after two days of orientation I would get my uniform, truck and all the tools I needed for the job. Needless to say when he said it was mandatory for me to work on Saturdays, I knew that the job would never be mine. I explained to him that I put on the application that I belonged to a Hebrew Pentecostal Church and we observed the seventh day Sabbath. He said I saw that but I didn't really understand what it meant, but we want you to know the job is yours if you can come in and even give us some Saturdays. Of course I had to tell him I appreciated him giving me the opportunity but I would not be able to accept the position.

I did find a job in Blue Island, at Blue Electric, which was about 10 minutes from Harvey where I lived. Blue Electric made commercial type freezers and furnaces. They did a lot of work for NASA. I learned how to read schematics while in school. A schematic is an electrical diagram of how electrical components work. With my training I had no problem getting this job. It was a fairly good paying job with benefits and vacations. I worked there for 2 years. Unfortunately, what happened to me in Pennsylvania caught up to me in Illinois. It was bought out by a corporation that does nothing but buy other companies for the sole purpose of taking them over, shutting them down and having access to their 401k and pensions. I thank the Lord that I was able to get my own apartment and a nice car before they went out of business. For about 6 or 7 months all I did was collect my unemployment and I did side jobs, painting, paper hanging and some electrical work. We did a lot of traveling with the pastor while working with him in his ministry.

The church was in Robbins, Illinois. We use to go to Fort Wayne, Indiana and fellowship with Bishop Jerry Carter. We made quite a few trips to Lexington, Kentucky. We fellowshipped with the late Bishop A. W. Morison who was the state superintendent. We kept busy in the ministry fellowshipping with other churches. After about 7 months my unemployment began to run out. Bishop Rich had a job with a tire company where they fixed a lot to truck tires. He was able to get me a job there, working with him. The job started off making $5 an hour. You've heard the expression that a half a loaf is better than nothing, well this wasn't even half a loaf, but you do what you have to do. Sometimes we feel like we are above certain jobs but when you don't have anything coming in its better than sitting there waiting for something to happen. If you can recall when I was in the church in Pennsylvania I had a skill of paper hanging, painting and putting up paneling. I used that skill to make extra money on Sundays. The Late Bishop Morison kept me busy, either working in his home or at the church. There were other people I worked for so I had a side job to fall back on to compensate for the salary I was making.

Sometimes you have to accept what you can get. A half a loaf is better than having nothing at all coming in. Yes, it is kind of hard sometimes when you are so use to making good money. I drove trucks, doubles, triples, hauling steel, worked in an automotive plant built trains for a period of time and I made good money. But at this point in my life jobs were really scarce. But I was really blessed because I had more to fall back on other than just painting on the weekend. I was very good at troubleshooting air conditioners, furnaces, and refrigerators and things of that nature. I had this friend of mine that I went to school with, a caucasian fellow. He was maybe a couple of years older than me. We graduated together went through the entire 12 months together. When he finished he started his own business and sometimes he would call me on Sundays to help him out.

The Lord had truly blessed me that I had a lot I could fall back on. I remember when we were in school during the football season he made a bet that Denver would walk all over Washington. If you remember the Washington Redskins had this black quarterback named Doug Williams and Denver had John Elway. As far as the odd makers were concerned Doug Williams was like a nobody compared to John Elway. No way was he supposed to win that game. But everybody who follows football knows what happened.

The bottom line is that even with a $5 an hour job I was still able to support my kids back east, keep my own place, and pay my tithes and offering.

When I was in Chicago I really had no social life. My social life consisted of working and going to church. On Saturday nights I would be in my room watching Saturday Night Sing. I conducted myself as a married man even though I was living by myself. Elder Rich had a lot of problems in the Robbins church. He was faced with a lot of folks that did not agree with the method in which the church was being run or didn't like the way he was preaching. You could always feel the tension in the church. It was like two churches in one building. This went on for at least a couple of years that I was there. A lot of disagreement, bad feelings, just wasn't the type of atmosphere one wanted to be in, especially in the church. So he elected to leave the church there in Robbins and rent a building in Chicago on Ashland Avenue, myself and some of the other members went with him. He was up for being a Bishop that year and according to the church by-laws, any man or woman who is charged to pastor a church cannot leave that position until the end of the convocation year. He didn't want to wait until the end of the year and therefore he could not become a Bishop at that time. He pastored in Chicago after leaving Robbins for about a year and a half.

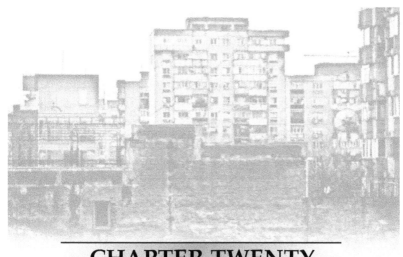

CHAPTER TWENTY

RELOCATED TO DETROIT WHERE MY MOTHER DIES

Then there came another opportunity for him to pastor in Detroit Michigan at the Buchanan Street church, where the great Lady Dentson was a member. Her husband who we called the bible scholar, Bishop Denison was the founder and pastor of this church. So he got the opportunity to go there and pastor, naturally I chose to go with him. By this time I had left my $5 an hour job and took a job driving a school bus. I worked for this company on Michigan Avenue where 95% of the business was charters. I took people to work and took school children on trips. I was doing pretty well financially. When I decided to move to Michigan, I started looking for a job about a month before he was to relocate. I had an aunt who lived in Detroit. I spent a weekend with her, went to church on Buchanan Street and looked for a job. The following Monday not only did I find a job but I also found a house to rent. My point is when I moved to Detroit not only did I have a job but also I had a place to live. Since I had been working in Chicago for this fellow driving the school bus, I had a CDL, good driving record, so I started looking for a job at bus companies. I found this black owned and operated company in Detroit on Nichols Street, Safeway Bus Company. I filled out the application and the next day I went back for orientation, did a blood test and all my paperwork in 4 days. Went back to Chicago and worked; two weeks later I heard from the company that upon arriving to Detroit I had a job to go to. Even the house I looked at was available before I came back to Detroit. I moved to Detroit on a Sunday and moved in to my house and started my job that Monday. I never could understand how people can say they can't find work. If you want a job there's a job out there for you. It may not be what you want but it's better than nothing. Now the church in Detroit, Michigan was as different as day and night, compared to the church in Robbins.

It reminded me of the church I came up in, in Norristown Pennsylvania. The people there were loving, spirit filled people, that came together for two reasons, to worship God and give him the glory. It was a place that you looked forward to going to. Unlike Illinois you had to pray before you went in that God would keep you and help you endure the things that were said and done in the church. There were not a whole lot of members but the anointing was there every weekend. I am a firm believer that if the anointing is not in the service you are not having church. Speaking for myself if I am in a service and I do not feel the anointing of God, the real presence of God then I don't want to be in the service. I've been in places where people are making up their own anointing and their own presence of the Lord. If you are filled with the Holy Ghost and you've gotten it like the bible says then you'll know without a shadow of a doubt if the anointing is real or if the folks are just putting on.

Everyone that is dancing and speaking in tongues does not have what they are confessing to have. The Bible says they have a form of godliness but denying the power thereof. After about a year and a half I clearly remember taking my mother downtown to this hospital for her quarterly checkup. They told her she had a lump on her chest. She was very disturbed by the finding. They didn't tell her if it was cancerous or not but she was clearly upset. In about a couple of weeks we found out that it was cancer. They told her that they had given her a year. Well we continued to go to church and give God the glory.

I'll never forget how in that year's time I saw her go from 180 pounds down to 60. After the first three and a half months of her chemo it came to a point where she could not even swallow. They instructed me to put all her food in a blender. We did that for a while until the doctor gave her a prescription. The prescription was for can food that was loaded with calories. Still, week, after week, after week. she insisted that I carry her down the steps, put her in the car and take her to church. She used a walker to go in and out of the church but she didn't have enough strength in her legs to go up and down the steps. It's hard to explain how hard it was for me, and when you think about it, it was equally as hard for her. I think in her last days we both tried to encourage each other. I tried not to let her know how it was affecting me feeling helpless, and she tried not to let me know how she felt going through what she was going through. I think I drew more strength from her than she drew from me. When I look back to the time I first came into the church, when I was saved and called to the ministry in her eyes I was a hero or a champion. She was so proud and happy when she spoke to her friends and neighbors. "This is my son the preacher, the minister." I remember this one particular day, as I stood in the kitchen, over the tray I had prepared to take upstairs I became overwhelmed with grief, tears started flowing. It reminded me of how I felt before I had a God on my side and in that point in my life I had hit rock bottom, leaning up against the pole as rain began to fall wondering how I got here. Back then I was shedding tears because I needed help and didn't know where it was coming from, but this time it was different I was shedding tears for my mother whom I loved dearly.

I was shedding tears because she needed help and I was faced with the truth that help wasn't coming it was just a matter of time. I thought about how she tried to protect me from knowing how much suffering she was going through. Sometimes I could hear her at night moaning and I would go in and say, "Ma Dear are you alright?" We grew up calling her Ma Dear long before Tyler Perry came out with his plays about Madea. I don't recall which one of my brothers started calling her Ma Dear because I was the last child born.

Towards her last days because she had the aid card, they assigned a nurse to come in and do whatever it is they do. We thanked God for that. She went to church week after week, sitting there sometimes in pain. At lunch time she couldn't eat. She use to tell the mothers of the church, and a lot of the elderly people during testimony service, Don't you all worry about me because I'll be fine." The last time she was in a hospital, Pastor Rich and I went together to see her. We walked in and before we could get in the room we could hear her singing. We knew what song she was singing but Pastor Rich asked her anyway. She said, "Nearer my God to Thee" and started laughing. We couldn't stay long we just went to check on her, there were nurses and doctors in and out of the room. We left and the very next time I came back that week would have been the very last time I saw her alive. I remember being in the room and some of the nurses had a procedure they had to do and they asked me to leave out. I said, "Ma Dear I'm going to be going, I'll see you later." It seems like her eyes began to water up. I didn't think about it until probably the next day. It was like she knew that we would never see each other again.

As I began to walk to the elevator, no more than 30 feet away, it seemed like it took forever. When I got halfway to the elevator I heard a lady on the intercom yelling code blue and a bell started going off. The elevator opened and people started running towards me. I didn't have to look back to see where they were going. I've seen enough doctor movies to know that code blue means someone was about to flat line or had already flat line. Everything was in slow motion, the door opened in slow motion and the people ran by me in slow motion. The only thing that was in normal speed was the lady on the intercom saying code blue. I believe I was in a state of denial not wanting to accept what was happening. I don't remember driving home that day. I just felt numb walking into the house and it was by telephone I found out that my mother had passed.

I believe she died before I even got back to the house.

ROMANS 8:28 Says *"All things works together for the good, to them that loves the Lord."* Even in her death and suffering she was able to touch somebody who didn't know GOD. The same young doctor that first diagnosed her one year earlier, called me one day before we had her homegoing service. He said I'd like to visit your church. He said not long ago she told me she was not afraid to die because she knew where she was going. He said I never seen anybody demonstrating the type of faith she had. For the saints in Michigan, we had a viewing. After that we flew her body down south to Newberry South Carolina. The church that my mother grew up in many years ago was still there and they had a cemetery in the back of the church. There was a plot for her to be buried in. One of her sisters, who made the arrangements, told me that she would be buried on Saturday.

I informed her that my mother was a Sabbath keeper. Not only would my mother not approve it. Don't expect me to be there. She called me back two days later and said we changed it. It will not be on Saturday. Naturally, I was extremely glad to hear that. They also allowed Bishop Rich to preach her homegoing service. The time came for us to load up in his van. His wife and children came with us. We met up with my brothers Tyrone and Joey down south. I also carried one of my mother's favorite mantles. Once we arrived at the undertakers in South Carolina, I gave the mantle to elect Lady Rich. She instructed the undertaker how to place it on my mothers' head. She was in a beautiful white dress and had her white mantle on as though she was on her way to church.

CHAPTER TWENTY-ONE

MOVED TO JERSEY AND CALLED TO PASTOR

After a year or so, Bishop Rich decided that he wanted to move back to Norristown, Pennsylvania and start another church. I never understood why he decided to do that. It came as a total surprise to all of us. But one thing was for sure, I was not about to follow him back to Norristown, Pennsylvania. I had originally left Norristown to work with him in his ministry. After a couple of years, he left Robbins, Illinois and went to Chicago and started a church. After a few years there, he decided to take a position in Detroit, Michigan. Again I relocated and moved to Detroit. So I was not going to follow him back to Pennsylvania, but when I think about it even this was in the plan of God. Because, for some time the Almighty has been dealing with me to launch out into the deep. Which means to pastor a church. But I wasn't willing to say yes to him. So I called my brother Joey. He use to live in Germantown, Philadelphia not far from Apostle Frazier a good friend of mine. After living with this woman for about 15 years, they decided to get married and they brought a farm in New Jersey. A place called Williamstown, about 30 miles from Atlantic City. I spoke to him about me staying there temporarily. He and his wife said they would love to have me come and stay with them until I got my own place. Just like the time I moved to Detroit, it took me less than a week to find a job.

I had a C.D.L license. If you remember, I drove buses in Chicago and Detroit. I didn't drive school buses right away. I went down to Atlantic City and found a job driving coaches. All of the casinos in Atlantic City had what they refer to as line runs. I was working from Sunday night Till Thursday morning and had Friday and Saturday off. My job consisted of picking up an empty coach every night and drive over to Philadelphia. I was picking up people in different places throughout the city. I would take them back to New Jersey and drop them off at different casinos. Sometimes, early Sunday mornings, they would have me go to the airport in Atlantic City and pick up people going to the casinos.

I was making pretty good money driving coaches. I had no problem paying my brother room and board. I was still able to support my children as well as save money. I was going to Bishop Hamilton church in Atlantic City. Maybe once a month I would drive to Norristown to visit my old church. I use to pass this little red and white church. I stopped one day and spoke to the pastor to find out if it was for sale. Because

I knew that God was calling me to pastor a church. It just so happened on this day when I stopped the pastor was cutting the grass. He told me this building was for sale and offered to take me inside. I fell in love with this place. I didn't have one person that was committed to be a part of the ministry that I was believing God for. My outreach ministry consisted of passing out tracks on the boardwalk and witnessing to family and friends.

By this time, my children where all young adults. My youngest son had joined the Marines. My daughter married someone who was in the army. The other two children were living with their girlfriends. We stayed in touch by phone. We could not spend as much time together as I would have liked to. Again, I knew without a shadow of a doubt, I was meant to pastor. Twenty-two years had passed since the day I came home and found my house completely empty. Of those twenty-two years, my wife was only with me two of those years after I bought a house for her to come back to. So you do the math. I am a living witness that God is a keeper. With the Lord's help I conducted myself as though I was still married.

By this time, it had become apparent to me that I had to start seeking God for an answer. If I was going to pastor a church, I would need a helpmate. So I began to ask God to send me a wife that loves him more than she loves' herself. I knew if I had a wife that loves God more than herself, she would be the perfect helpmate for me. So, I began to seek the Lord in prayer and fasting. I prayed and I prayed and I prayed. I knew that God would answer my prayers. It was about 7 weeks after I started asking God for a wife. He brought someone to my mind. It was one individual that came to my mind that believed as I believed. For the Bible teaches not to be unequally yoked. This person was in Chicago, Illinois and for about 3 years we were in the same church. When I was in the church in Robbins, Illinois, she was still married. I was conducting myself as though I was still married. We never said too much to each other, other than hello, goodbye and praise the Lord. My social life consisted of working and going to church. It never occurred to me that someday I would be considering her for a wife. Her husband had died before I moved from Detroit, Michigan. So, according to the Bible that made her free to remarry again.

But, in my case, even with the divorce, my children's mother was still alive. There were some people telling her not to marry me. I remember something the late Bishop Rollins told me years ago. "It's one thing to live in it, but it's another to die in it." Not to get ahead of myself, I remember after much prayer, giving her a call. I told her that I was planning to come to the Chicago area, and I would be visiting the church in Robbins, Illinois. I never revealed to her my reason for coming. She called me back about a week later and said her pastor wanted me to be the keynote speaker for that day. I told her that I would love to preach that weekend.

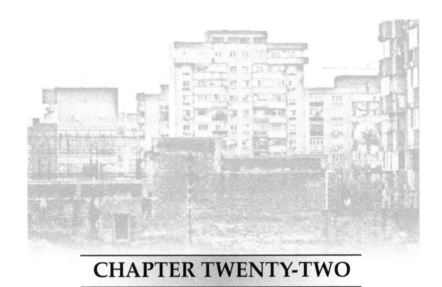

CHAPTER TWENTY-TWO

I Proposed To Her While She Sat On A Swing

In a couple of weeks, I was at the airport in Chicago. She met me at the airport and dropped me off at the hotel in Harvey. We had a wonderful service that Sabbath day. My subject was, "The hedge is down but God is in control" coming from the book of Job. After the service was over, I took her out to dinner. She had no idea that I was there to see if she would consider to allow me to court her. It would have to be by phone because we lived in two different states. She looked at me with a smile on her face and politely said the Lord may have spoken to you about considering her for a wife, but he has not said anything to me. So I guess you could say she turned me down in a nice way. She also said I'm flattered but not interested. She said I like you as a person and a man of God because you've always treated me with the utmost respect. She smiled at me again and said but a courtship I'm not interested in. The next day, I flew back to Philadelphia, PA and rented a car at the airport and drove back to Jersey. I waited about a month and decided to write her a letter. I wrote a three page letter with some original poetry. One of the things that I said was "Love is not love until it has been given away" and I also said "A song is not a song until it has been signed." In the letter, I jokingly said if you keep turning me down I'd probably end up in Africa doing missionary work. Little did I know, some 15 years later, the Lord would do just that and send me to Africa.

Seven weeks had passed since I sent the letter. Then one Sunday evening about 7 o'clock, I received a phone call, when I heard her voice saying "Hello Elder Harris," I became extremely happy and thankful. She said, I've been praying over this letter and I don't think it would be any harm if we called each other from time to time. We did that two or three times a week. Some weeks we spoke every day. I was feeling pretty good about where the conversations were going. We found that we had so much more in common than just our religious beliefs. I let her know the Lord was calling me to pastor a church. We talked about the type of ministry that we both would like to be involved with.

After about two months of us talking on the phone, she asked me if I could come back to Chicago for a weekend. I said I would love to. Within a couple of weeks I was on a plane bound for Chicago. Once I arrived at the airport I decided to take the bus to Harvey. I didn't know it at the time, but she wanted me to go to her oldest daughter house so that her three daughters could have a conversation with me. After the service, we went to her daughter house. I met with Sheron, Beverly, and Tiffany. At least an hour while I sat next to their mother on the sofa, they all took turns asking me questions. Before we left, they all thanked me for answering all their questions. They did not tell me if they approved of me or not. One thing is for sure, in the hour that I set there, it was the longest hour of my life.

After we left the daughter's house, we went out to dinner. We had a real good conversation about our future. It was at dinner, I invited her to come to New Jersey to meet my family and my former pastor. She agreed to come and spend a few days with us. When she arrived at the airport, I picked her up and took her to a nice hotel in Williamstown, New Jersey about 10 minutes from where I lived. I took her to the church I came up in. The next day, which was Sunday, we had a barbecue in New Jersey. I wanted her to meet all of my family.

In the front of my brothers' house was a huge oak tree. The tree had a swing on it. I asked her to sit on it while I pushed her from the back. After a while, I stopped the swing and walked around to the front of her. As I took the ring box out of my pocket, I knelt down on one knee and asked her if she would marry me.

Her answer was yes! Her flight was to leave early Tuesday morning. So Sunday evening, I took her to Atlantic City with me. I wanted to give her a tour of Philadelphia and show her what my job consist of. I left work about 30 minutes early so we could stop in South Philly for one of those famous Philly Cheesesteaks from Pats Steak. She was having a wonderful time being chauffeured in a brand new coach. It was just me and her all the way to Philadelphia. When I arrived at my first pickup, I told her to sit behind me and pretend to be just another passenger. I got her back to the hotel Monday morning. I went straight home. We both got plenty of rest. I picked her up at 4 o'clock Monday afternoon. We went to my former pastor's house, Mother Sessoms, to receive some good counseling.

CHAPTER TWENTY-THREE

SATAN TRIES TO TAKE MY LIFE AGAIN

We arrived at Mother Sessoms house and needless to say, Mother Sessoms was very happy and excited for both of us. Because she knew how many years I have gone without a wife, we were not in a hurry to set a date for the wedding. At this point of our lives we were mostly talking about the ministry the Almighty was going to place us over. She knew that God was calling me to pastor. By her being a licensed minister she would be the co-founder and co-pastor. For a couple of months, we talked mostly about the church. In our organization, you became a pastor by either being sent out by the headquarter church in Lexington, Kentucky or have a few people that believe as you believe and are willing to follow you. As I said before, there was not one committed person in Jersey willing to follow me as I follow Christ.

But, on the other hand, we both come to realize there were people in Chicago who would be part of the ministry. I became convinced in our conversations after discussing the church for two months, perhaps it isn't that little red and white church in Jersey the Lord wants me to pastor. I began to feel like he was leading me to Chicago. There were people who would be willing from day one be a part of the church in Illinois. We did not have a building to conduct services in. My fiancée reminded me that her house has a full basement. Many people have started churches in their basements.

We talked about the possibility of it if I elected to move to Chicago. Shortly after that conversation, I told my fiancée that God had confirmed to me that Chicago is where he wants me to pastor. Not long after I shared that with her, I was going to Norristown for service. I was on the expressway when the Lord began to speak to me, just like he did over 22 years ago, when I was leaning against that pole, contemplating suicide.

I heard the Lord say what you are about to do will be permanent but the problem is temporary.

So, here I am on I-76 westbound and God says to me the name of the church will be "The Cornerstone House of God." The wedding date was set and I was to arrive in Chicago two weeks before the wedding. I was supposed to stay at deacon and sister Banks house. Sister Banks was my fiancée best friend. Now, when I was all packed up and headed for Chicago, I was driving a small Toyota pickup truck and I had a U-Haul trailer hooked up to the back of the truck. I had a 25-inch television sitting on the seat next to me. Satan tried again to take my life. But thanks be to God again he failed. I know what David meant when he said in the hundred and twenty-four division of Psalms, "If it had not been the Lord who was on our side." I remember stopping at a service area in the mountains of Pennsylvania at night. The houses look like little tiny lights as you look down because you are so high above sea level. When I came through the last tunnel, I had been driving for at least 5 hours straight.

I stopped for a cup of coffee and to call my fiancée. I set there for about 15 minutes talking to her and then got back on the road. I didn't find out until a couple days later she felt troubled in her spirit. She called sister Banks who also is one of her prayer partners and she said I feel a need to pray for James. I thank God for her being obedient to the spirit of God. Not long after I had gotten back on I-76 going west, there was this car coming up behind me traveling over a hundred miles per hour. I never saw his light coming up behind me but I heard a big boom. I remember being pushed forward at a high rate of speed as though I was being shot out of a cannon.

I was headed towards the cliff. The impact was so hard, that it pushed the small truck that I was driving and the U-Haul trailer I was pulling over the railing and down the cliff. This took place about 30 minutes after speaking to my fiancée. I believe it was in that 30 minutes of prayer, they were able to bind the enemy. The truck had broken lose from the trailer I was pulling. The trailer went one way and I went tumbling down the hill. At this point, it seemed like everything was in slow motion. The last time I experienced something like this was when my mother passed in Detroit. I could hear the metal scraping and hitting up against the rocks as the truck continued to roll over and over. Each time the truck rolled over, I remember saying, "Jesus." I did not know if I was going to be pierced with metal or if the truck was going to blow up as it continued to rollover and slide down the hill. I could see sparks flying and hear metal as it hit up against the rocks over and over. I felt as though I was about to die. I just didn't know how. I thought perhaps the truck would blow up. Somewhere between the top of the cliff and the bottom, I must have lost consciousness. I could not remember how I got out of the truck. But, I do recall just before reaching the top, crawling on my hands and knees.

Once I reached the top, I fell flat on my face and then rolled over on my back. Suddenly, a lady appeared out of nowhere and said to me, "You're going to be alright. I'm going to stay with you." That's all I remembered. Apparently I had lost consciousness again. Before I opened my eyes again, I could hear people talking. Someone said he has lost a lot of blood. They began to cut my clothes off. That's probably why parts of my shirt and pants felt damp. They were soaked in blood. They were trying to find out where I was bleeding. I knew I was covered in my own blood. As they began to place me in the ambulance, I asked where is the woman that was here and who is she?

I was told that no one else was here when they arrived. They said someone traveling east bound had called 911 and reported seeing a vehicle going off a cliff at this mile marker. Nobody seems to know where the lady came from or where she went. I don't believe that a trucker just happened to be going by at the exact time I was being pushed over a cliff. But I do believe God had a couple of angels up there in the mountains with me. The Almighty truly blessed me that night. I had no broken bones and no long lasting injury. I did encounter a lot of long cuts on my arms and back that I probably will have for the rest of my life. The next time I woke up, I was in the hospital. I was told at that time I had been thrown out of the truck, because where they found the truck was at the bottom of the cliff. There is no way I could have climbed back to where they found me. The night of the accident they called my brother in Jersey and two days later he was there to pick me up.

CHAPTER TWENTY-FOUR

THE WEDDING TAKES PLACE AND WE HONEYMOON IN NIAGARA FALLS

When I got back to New Jersey, I called Chicago to let everyone know that I would be catching a flight on Thursday of next week. I would get there four days before the wedding as opposed to two weeks before the wedding. Before my brother and I went back to Jersey, we went to the auto graveyard where they towed the truck. I wanted to see what I could salvage. We looked at the truck and what was left of the 25-inch television that was sitting in the front seat next to me. We both knew that it took a miracle for me to live through that wreck.

Eventually, I did make it to Chicago by plane. Our daughters, Sheron, Beverly, and Tiffany were the wedding planners. They did an excellent job. My wife and I could not ask for a better wedding. It was held at her old church in Robbins, IL. For our honeymoon, we went to Niagara Falls. We stayed at a hotel in Chicago that Sunday and flew to Buffalo, New York that Monday and rented a car. The next day, we went to the other side of the Falls into Canada. We were having the time of our life. When that Friday came, it was an extremely long day. Walking, shopping, and sightseeing really took a toll on both of us. That night, which was Friday, she asked me what are we doing tomorrow and I said what we do every Sabbath day, go to church. We had a car that we rented at the airport, so we drove over to Toronto, Canada where some of our churches are located. I knew Bishop Clock so we decided to spend the Sabbath with him. We had a wonderful time with the saints there in Toronto. Saturday night we had a lovely dinner. After dinner, we went down to the Falls and sat on a bench and watched the water come over the falls. At night, they have these huge spot lights that are different colors that create a beautiful atmosphere. We sat there for nearly two hours cuddled up thinking about the Lord discussing our future and enjoying each other. After about 9 days of being on a wonderful honeymoon, we headed back to Chicago and got busy in the ministry. We started having service in the basement.

We live in a suburban town about 35 miles south of Chicago. My wife worked for the city that we lived in. I was going to a chiropractor because of the accident that occurred on my way to Chicago. The fellow who pushed me off that cliff had insurance coverage that paid for all my medical expenses along with a cash settlement. I was able to go back to work 3 months after the accident driving a coach for a company in

Chicago. I did a lot of charters mostly taking people to casinos that were in Chicago and Indiana.

CHAPTER TWENTY-FIVE

My Wife is Arrested and Taken To Jail!

On this particular day, I picked up a group in Chinatown in Chicago and took them to the casino in Joliet, Illinois. Our pickup was at 5am in the morning, arriving at the casino at 7am and be loaded back up at 12pm headed back to Chinatown. Well, I had the coach loaded and just about ready to pull off when I received this terrifying phone call. It was my wife on the other end. She was screaming James come home as soon as you can. I'm on my job and I'm going to be arrested and taken to jail. Now, let me just backup for a few minutes and tell you why I was concerned about her safety. I had mentioned that she works for the city and there was a lot of corruption taking place in this town. You know how it is when new administration comes into an office after the election they try to get jobs for people that supported them.

We believe that the mayor who was just elected wanted my wife's job for someone else. They did everything they could to get her off of that job. They knew that she kept the Sabbath and did not work on Friday nights. She had enough seniority to stay on the day shift. But, somehow they managed to get her on the 2nd shift. The union advised her to use her sick days if she did not want to work on Friday nights. It would take 30 days for the union to settle her case through arbitration. She used about 5 of her sick days by the time the union convinced the city she had enough seniority to stay on the day shift. But, they didn't stop there. They had a police commander and her supervisor to make up some lies that would lead to her arrest and consequently her job.

The city's cars and trucks are kept in an enclosed parking lot. Her supervisor and this police commander were in the parking garage when she came in. She did not feel comfortable being there by herself. She said to them, "I was just about to leave." She began to drive out. She heard the supervisor yell, "She just hit me." My wife proceeded outside and parked the truck and called me. We both knew they were staging this accident. I told her to stay calm. I was calling some people to get to the police station real soon. Then I heard her say, "A police car just pulled up behind me." I told her to keep the phone on and let him know you're speaking to your husband. I heard him say are you Betty Harris? She said yes I'm speaking to my husband right now. I was surprised he did not tell her to turn the phone off. He said to her, "We got a call that you left the scene of an accident." Then he said, "Can you step out of the car and put your hands behind you?" Then the phone went off. I called the FBI. I'm sure right about now this is beginning to sound pretty farfetched. Why would I call the FBI? Why not call the state police? I really don't know what processed me to call them. I knew I felt completely helpless and was concerned about my wife safety and well being.

When I finally got a chance to speak to one of the agents, he asked me what town did you say the police station was in? When I mentioned the name of the town again he said hold on I'm going to let you speak to the agent working that area. Evidently there was already an investigation taking place regarding this town. So when he picked up the phone he just asked me one question, "her name." He said I'm going to call them now and let them know I'm coming to speak to her. He said I will probably be there when you arrive. I made it to the police station in about 2 hours. Which was pretty good considering I had started from Joliet and drove to Chinatown and back to the south side. When I walked into the police station, the waiting area was jammed packed. I'm talking about standing room only. I had been making calls all the way to Chicago and back. All the kids were there. Some of the grandkids also came. Member from our church, the late Bishop A.W. Morrison came as well as members from other churches. They all came to show their support. As I was talking to some of the people there, I heard someone say "There's Pastor Harris standing near the water fountain." When I turned around, I saw a young African American man coming towards me. It turned out to be the FBI agent I spoke to. He was in his early 40's wearing sneakers, brown slacks and a Temple University sweat shirt. He came over and introduced himself to me and said, "I spoke to your wife and she's doing as well as can be. You will have to wait until tomorrow to post bail." I thanked him for coming and for all that he had done. I also had a lawyer come out and speak to her that night. Before we all left, the mayor of the town showed up. He probably was concerned about why the FBI wanted to speak with her. So the day when my wife came home, we found out they charged her with six different things. The most serious charges were leaving the scene of an accident. Because of the type of charges, we needed a good criminal lawyer. We heard about a Jewish lady who was supposed to be a good criminal lawyer. Her office was on the 14th floor downtown on Michigan Avenue across from the Art Institute. Because of the lawsuit we were bringing up against the city, the case dragged on for 5 long years. After about 3 years, her lawyer suggested it might be better for her to plead guilty on the lesser charges. Naturally because she knew she was innocent, she refused to plead guilty to anything the day before the final trial came.

I organized a picket line in front of the Markham courthouse. I knew the press would be there because I called them. All of the signs said "gang bangers in high places." I had a sign, some of the kids had signs as well as some church members. The next day was to be the final arguments between our lawyers and then the verdicts. We told everyone on this day we wanted to be by ourselves. Court started at 8:30. At 11:40 it was over. It was now in the hands of six men and six women. They went out at 11:40 am and came back at 5:50 pm. They had us to stand up and on all of the charges we heard them say, "NOT GUILTY – NOT GUILTY – NOT GUILTY – NOT GUILTY – NOT GUILTY – NOT GUILTY."

CHAPTER TWENTY-SIX

WE BOTH EXPERIENCED A LOT OF DEATH IN OUR FAMILIES

The one thing that stood out in my mind concerning the trial, as soon as the judge dismissed us, the 12 men and women that gave us the verdict left the court room. My wife and I did not leave right away. The judge wanted to congratulate her and we talked to the lawyer. But, when we finally got downstairs and into the parking lot, all 12 of the people that brought in that verdict was waiting in the parking lot. They wanted to congratulate my wife. In about a year, the city came to a settlement with my wife regarding the lawsuit she brought against them. Shortly after that case was settled, she decided to take an early retirement.

We had only been married for about a year when her mother passed away. Shortly after that her sister husband passed away. James was a quartet singer. When he wasn't in church he would be fishing or someplace singing with his group.

Then there was her oldest brother in Detroit. He rehabbed houses for a living. He was on a ladder one day and fell off. When she got to Detroit he was in intensive care. She stayed up there for a few days. She said I came home because the Lord told me that he was going to be alright. A couple of days later, she got a call letting her know that her brother had passed away. She had a hard time coping with that because she knew God told her that he would be alright. But, Later she come to understand and realize when the Almighty speaks to us we assume that it means one thing when it could mean something entirely different. At first she was thinking God was going to heal him and bring him home. On the contrary, God was comforting her by saying he is in a better place.

Both of my brothers passed away within one year's time. I was cutting the grass one Sunday on my riding lawnmower, when I noticed my wife standing on the porch with a cordless phone in her hand. I went over and answered the phone. It was my sister in-law telling me my brother was at the VA Hospital. The next day I was picking up a rental car at the Philadelphia International Airport. I went straight to the hospital in West Philadelphia. I stayed at a hotel in Norristown and I traveled back and forth for 4 days witnessing to him.

Neither one of us knew when I prepared to leave that Thursday afternoon it would be the last time I would see him alive. I said, "Joey it's time for me to go but I'll be talking to you soon." He couldn't speak at the time but with his right hand he gave me a thumbs up sign. He had a smile on his face and his eyes began to water up. Just one week later on a Sunday again I was riding my lawnmower and my wife came out on the porch holding the cordless phone. I stopped what I was doing an answered the phone. Have you ever had that eerie feeling that you have done this the exact same way? It was my brother Joey wife again telling me that my brother had just passed away. In a couple of days, I was back in New Jersey. Because he was a veteran, the funeral was held in a chapel at a cemetery exclusively for veterans. They had the blowing of the Taps, the shooting of the rifles as they stood in full dress uniforms, and the flag that draped his casket was folded up and presented to his wife.

As sad as this occasion was, it was a time for the children to be proud of him the way the military was putting their father to rest. In just about 7 months later, I received a totally unexpected call from West Philadelphia, PA. It was my oldest brother wife telling me that he had just passed away. The reason it was unexpected is because I just spoke to him last Sunday. Even though I lived in Chicago we both are die hard Philadelphia Eagles fans. We called each other every Sunday. I knew he was on disability because of some health issues, but he wasn't feeling sick last week. I remember asking him if he was still going to the church around the corner. He said God has been too good to me for me not to go. I was told that he became sick late Monday night and had to be rushed to the hospital. He was put in intensive care on Wednesday, by Friday afternoon complications had set in and 5:30 Sunday he passed away. I told her I will not make my flight reservations until she let me know when the funeral will be.

She called me back Monday night and said the funeral will be Saturday. Needless to say this did not sit well with me at all because she knew the stand that I had taken when my mother died. She was at my mother's homegoing service. I made it very clear if they had it on Saturday, I will not be there. Sometimes people will do things to see if you will bend in your religious beliefs! She called me back Tuesday night and said, "hi Jimmy we have a problem. We did not have the insurance long enough for them to cover the funeral." I asked her, "Is it still going to be on Saturday?" She said yes. I said to her, "We don't have a problem. You have a problem!" I politely said gsoodbye!

CHAPTER TWENTY-SEVEN

STARTED SEVERAL BUSINESSES

I worked on several different jobs before we started our own business. My first job was fixin truck tires. Then, I drove coaches for a company in Chicago. Then I drove a truck for a tree service company. My first company was in the medical transportation business. We purchased a slightly used 15 passenger van. We went to City Hall in downtown Chicago. We applied for the MC Plate there and started the corporation at the same time. We took some of the seats out and had a handicap lift installed. My wife did all of the bookkeeping. I drove the van. And I took the clients wherever they had to go. We were paid by the state once a month. We became so busy that my wife had to help out with some of the clients going to the hospital appointments. I basically took care of all of the wheelchair clients. For about two and a half years, things were really good. But, one day, we got a letter from the state of Illinois for all the vendors to come to Rosemont Illinois for a meeting regarding medical transportation in Illinois. The state wanted to privatize the work. We basically did the paperwork the same way, but we never knew when we were going to be paid. We continued the business for about 6 months. Then a friend of mine who also is a pastor, helped us to get into the school bus business. We were subcontractors. We started with one bus and ended up with 3. After about 4 years, I was talking to a fellow who owned a dump truck. I found out I could make with one truck what I made with three school buses.

So, getting out of the school bus business and going into the dump truck business was a no-brainer. The fella who convinced me that it was more profitable to have one dump truck as opposed to three school buses took me to the company he leased his truck to. It was the biggest cement company in Chicago. I stayed with this company for three years. The operating cost became too expensive. The cost of plates was more than doubled. Diesel fuel was going through the roof and the insurance had doubled. So I decided to get out of the business. I went back to work as a tractor trailer driver. After about three years, I retired and collected my pension and social security. My wife and I felt that if I retired I could be full time in the ministry. The church did keep us extremely busy. I often tell the people at the church the success of a ministry is not based on how many cars are in the parking lot or how many people are in the pew. It's based on what it does in the community. And if it's dealing with the hurts and needs

142

of the people. Most of all, is the anointing present. Healing comes through the anointing. Deliverance comes through the anointing. The Apostle Paul said, "But by the Grace of God I am what I am." The Lord has blessed our local church to be a blessing to the people in it. As well as the people in the communities around it. What we have been able to do is by The Grace of God.

We have been referred to as the little church with a big heart! Just to mention some of the things God has blessed us to do in our outreach ministries from the very beginning. When I used to have school buses, I would take a bus once a week to the food pantry and bring it back loaded with food. Deacon Alexander would help me to unload the school bus on Friday afternoon Then we distributed the food on Sunday morning. In the early part of our ministry, we were on Cable TV. We also had a nursing home ministry. We would go to the nursing homes and have service there. By the Grace of God, we also had outreach ministry in other cities. When I had my semi, I would hook one to a flatbed, load up the church people in a school bus and we would go to Penbrook Illinois and have church outside. With me preaching on the flatbed. When we had a lot of young people, we had a boy scout charter.

We also by the Grace of God are still having a cedar program feeding about 35 children breakfast and lunch. We also are still currently by the Grace of God, giving dinners out on Thanksgiving Day. We don't have people coming to the church. What I normally do on the morning of Thanksgiving Day, is sit at my desk at the church and call the police stations in six different cities. I find out how many officers are working the morning and how many will be coming in on the afternoon shift. And we feed the people in lockup as well. So It could be anywhere between 15-30 dinners going to each one of the police stations. And the cities where the stations are located are Phoenix, Illinois, Posen, Illinois, Robbins, Illinois, Harvey Illinois, Markham Illinois and Country Club Hills, Illinois. As I take the orders, we have about six volunteers in the dining room fixing the dinners and putting them into boxes. Deacon Harris and my son, Minister Robert, would deliver them to the police stations.

We have been doing this for the past 18 years with the exception of 2013. We had a fire in our house four days before Thanksgiving. Our Insurance company put us in a hotel for two weeks. But we were blessed even with the house fire. You see the house caught on fire at 3 pm in the afternoon. If it had started at 3 am as we all slept, we all probably would have died in the fire. Everything the Almighty has allowed us to do I give him the Glory and Honor. Because, when you think about it, we can do nothing without him. And it's our reasonable service. I love God with all my heart, mind and soul and it's not because of what he has done or for what he's going to do. I love him just because he is.

CHAPTER TWENTY-EIGHT

FIRST MEETING WITH BISHOP ATSANGO

One of my favorite gospel song is, "I Am A Living Testimony." Because the Lord has given me 70 years of Testimonies. Testimonies of divine healing, divine deliverance, and divine protection. Testimonies of ways being made. And I'm so grateful and honored for all the things he has done for me. In the very beginning of my teenage years, I told you I had a job at the Flying A Gas Station and if you remember I had a rag for washing cars and it became my favorite rag to use. And this is how I feel about the Almighty God that I am serving. Just like that favorite rag I used to look for when I had a job to do. When God has a job for someone to do, I want him to look down and say, "there's my favorite rag." I have always made myself available to God and he has chosen me to travel to the other side of the world to represent the church. And, I am grateful. I will never forget how it all began. In the year of 2006, November, I remember being in my office listening to my messages on my phone. And there was a young man who said he was from Kenya, East Africa.

He could not explain a whole lot to me because you only have a certain amount of time to leave a message. But I remember he left the phone number of the hotel where he was staying. He said he was in the U.S. because he had been invited to a Mega church in the town where my church is located to run a conference. And he left the phone number, and I called him back, I think, the next day. And he wasn't in, but I left a message at the hotel to contact him and give him my cell phone number. He called me back on my cell phone the next day. And he said he would like to meet with me somewhere, perhaps at the church or if I could just come to the hotel and speak to him. He said that he had a Visa that was supposed to last for two months, but unfortunately, the people that had invited him to the U.S. were only paying for his hotel for one week.

So, therefore, he's in a country that he's never been in. He doesn't know anybody except for the people that invited him to come over and run the conference for five (5) days. And his hope was that the Lord would put somebody in his path to help him to be able to spend more time here He had no friends, very little money, even though he preached at this church all that week. He was hoping to be able to stay longer than just a week or two. So I told him that I would meet with him, and to make a long story short, the next day I went to my church on the southside of Chicago. I live in a place called Aroma Park in a subdivision outside of Kankakee, Illinois. And the church is some 35 miles North of Kankakee. So I told him that I would meet with him, and I did meet with him at the hotel. And I decided to take him to a buffet, early dinner someplace.

We went to a buffet diner, and needless to say, he was very impressed of the amount of food that was available to the people there, coming from Kenya and being raised up in some of the poorest areas in Africa. He wasn't accustomed to seeing so much food in one place at one time that you could eat all you wanted to eat. And we talked over dinner. And I was very impressed by this young man. By profession, he had gone to school and gotten a license to be a teacher. He was a teacher in Kenya for a number of years. And he also was an Overseer.

I think at this particular time, he had 20 churches under him. He has a wife and two daughters. He also had adopted four of his brother's children because his brother had died of AIDS. This is something that's running rampant over in Africa, the AIDS virus and all the other kinds of diseases that people catch over there. So he took in his brothers' four children along with his own. He has a big household, a big responsibility, as well as being the Overseer of 20 other pastors. And I became very interested in what he had to talk about because it seems that he had learned about the Sabbath and he had heard about Feast Days, and he wanted to know more about the Sabbath and Feast Days. And I know it was not an accident that he called me because he told me he went to the phone book and began to make calls. And he called several different churches and nobody got back to him. He left messages, and I was the only church that got back to him. But the reason he felt a connection between my local church and his was because the name of his church in Eldoret, East Africa, is Cornerstone International House of God. And the only difference between my church and his is the word " International." The name of my church is Cornerstone House of God. So he saw that in the phone book, and he called me and left a message.

And I was very excited about meeting with him, especially when he talked about how he had heard bout the Seventh Day Sabbath being right and that God had Feast Days He wanted the people in Kenya East Africa to learn of and consequently observe. So I invited him to stay. My wife and I talked about it before I went back to tell him that we wanted him to stay at my home for as long as his Visa would allow him to say in this country. We would be honored to have him as a guest in our home. And I used this opportunity during the two months that he stayed with us to teach him one-on-one about the statues of the Lord which are the Feast Day, Passover, Pentecost on up to the last Feast Day which is the Feast of Tabernacles.

We also spent time dealing with scriptures regarding the Seventh Day Sabbath. And he accepted all that we showed him. We showed him scriptures that he never really had a clear understanding about. For example, Jeremiah the tenth chapter verses one through four. He never understood what God was telling his people hundreds of years before the birth of Christ. I know it was nothing but God that brought us together. I believe it was in December of that same year, I carried him down to our headquarters' church in Lexington, KY. Once a year we have a national youth council. And churches from all over the United States and different places will come for this weekend convention. And I wanted him to meet our Chief Apostle James E. Embry and our assistant Chief Apostle T.E. Clark and the Director of all African Affairs, Apostle George E. Daley who has lived in Zimbabwe for some 13 years. And he was very excited about going to meet some of the other officials. And not only that, it was in this service he joined and became a part of the House of God. And in doing so, all of the other pastors and leaders that were under him were a part of the House of God headquarters located in Lexington, Kentucky. It was Apostle Clark that took him in. In the year of 2006 in December, once we were back in Illinois, we also took him around to different pastors and got him speaking engagements. He preached at one of our churches in Robbins, Illinois. He preached in Hammond, Indiana and for some pastors who are in different organizations, but good friends of mine. And each time he preached, he would receive a love offering. He would always send money back to his family back in Eldoret E. Africa which was a place that's about seven hours North of Nairobi. So he stayed with us for two months. And I had talked to Apostle Daley about the possibility of my going to Kenya to teach and run a conference for two weeks. And with all of his wisdom, he advised me that it would be better to allow him to go back and teach the people what he has learned and then wait for the invitation to come as opposed to just going over there and trying to teach something they would be hearing for the first time. And coming from somebody that they have never known or seen before.

CHAPTER TWENTY-NINE

MY FIRST TRIP TO KENYA EAST AFRICA

So I wisely elected to wait until the following year. And sure enough before the 2007 year was out, I had received a letter from Pastor Julius whom I had adopted as my son in the Gospel. And he wanted me to come over just before Passover for me to run a meeting. Teaching the feast days and the seven day Sabbath. Not only to the churches and pastors that were under him. But he had other churches from Nairobi and other parts of Kenya that wanted to come in and be a part of this conference. So, I thank God for that door being opened for me to go for my very first time in the year of 2007. I purchased my airline ticked over the phone. It was $3200 dollars round trip. And about 10 days before departure, I went to the hospital in Flossmoor, Illinois and received three needles in each one of my arms in addition to that I had to purchase $400 dollars worth of pills. These pills were to be taken three days before leaving and one every day after I arrive. But that's only the beginning of my expenses. You see my son doesn't have a car. So he tells me exactly how much it will cost to rent a car for 14 days. And he factors in how much gas will be used in that time. He also figures out how much the meals and hotel will cost in Nairobi E. Africa and the hotel in Eldoret as well.

So the day finally arrived for me to board the plane that will carry me to the other side of the world. To a place in my wildest imaginations, I never would have dreamed of going in Kenya East Africa! We arrived at the overseas terminal about 10:30 Sunday morning. At the O'Hare Airport almost feeling like I was going to wake up from a good dream. I've never been to college but if I had to describe the emotions and feelings I was having it would be like going off to college. I wasn't just grateful to be going to Africa, it was more about the reason I was going. The Almighty could have chosen anyone he wanted to but he chosen this little commandment keeper with a small church and a handful of members.

When Apostle Paul made the statement forgetting those things that are behind, he was not suggesting that we should forget where we came from. My wife had came inside with me and as I stood in line we hugged and kissed and said good-bye. It had taken about an hour and a half for me to make it through security and to get to my gate. Finally, time came for us to board the plane. It was the biggest plane I had ever been on. There were aisles on both sides of the plane. The back of each seat had a TV monitor and the food was surprisingly good. It took about 12 and a half hours to make it to London Heathrow Airport. It was a long but enjoyable and relaxing flight. We had a two hour layover in London and then we took off for Africa. We arrived there Monday evening. Just before the plane descended, I heard the captain say in a British accent, "Welcome to Nairobi East Africa. We will be on the ground in two minutes. Hope you had a nice flight and a pleasant stay in Kenya. Thank you for flying with us."

And then the fasten your seatbelt light came on. I put my seatbelt on and looked out the window. Nairobi looked like any other large city in the US from up here. But, because of what the captain just said, I knew that I did not have to pinch myself. I was in Africa and just like every city in the US it was just as hard and as long to get through customs. I had two forms to fill out to purchase a visa. After I obtained my visa, I went downstairs to reclaim my bags. After getting my bags, I still had one more custom line to go through. When I came through that line, I heard a woman's voice with a accent. She called out "Daddy." And when I turned around to look, I saw my son Julius and two women with him. The one who called me Daddy was his wife. We adopted Julius as our son in the gospel. So his wife is my daughter in-law. She calls me daddy and I called her my daughter in-law. The other young lady was his niece. She lives in Nairobi and Julius lives in Eldoret which is 7 hours north of Nairobi. Whenever they come to Nairobi they usually stay with her. Once we greeted each other we headed out for the city which was about 20 miles from the airport. The hotel where I stay was about 5 blocks from downtown Nairobi. Riding through the streets at night, I knew I was in a different country. The public transportations was mostly white vans with yellow stripes. They kept the side doors open and every so often you see people jumping in and out. And they had the strangest sounding horns I ever heard.

153

I noticed a large presence of solders with guns. About every few blocks you would see them on the corners. We also saw some military trucks with soldiers standing up in the back of them; it almost felt like being in a city that was being occupied by an army; it would take a couple of days before I would find out why there were a large amount of soldiers in the city. After checking in the hotel and getting my bags in my room, Julius and I came down to the dining room where his wife and niece were having a cup of tea.

The hotel was much nicer than I had expected. It reminded me of the old 1942 classic movie Casablanca starring Humphrey Bogart. All of the waiters and waitress were dressed in black and white. The men wore black pants, white shirts, black ties and black vests. The women wore black skirts, white blouses and a black vests. They all ordered baked fish and rice with mixed vegetables and a spicy red sauce on the rice. The fish was baked with the head still attached. I just settled for the chicken and rice. It was spicy but very good.

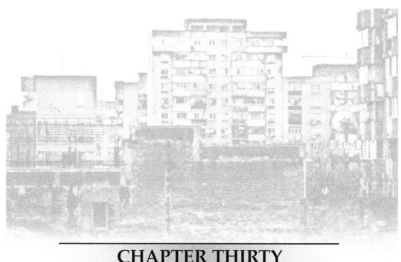

CHAPTER THIRTY

TEACHING CONFERENCE IN ELDORET EAST AFRICA

After dinner we all said goodnight because we had to leave early the next morning. It was a 7 hour drive to Eldoret where Julius lives. The rooms did not have a bathtub but it was a step in shower. It's more commonly known in Africa as a widow maker. It's an electric conduit that runs up the wall and is attached to a copper coil that hangs over the center of the shower. When you push a button outside the door the coil gets hot. And when you turn the water on that's over the heating coil the water becomes warm. I'm not an electrician but one thing I do know is water and electricity do not go well together, so I chose to take a cold shower. I was able to get a good night's sleep in spite of the sounds of the city. We call New York the Big Apple, the city that never sleeps. But I believe Nairobi East Africa should hold that title. The white and yellow public transportation vans with the crazy sounding horns we're blowing all night long. And if that wasn't enough, every 3 hours I heard what I believe to be a mosque's broadcast call to prayer from a loudspeaker. Even though I could not understand the language, it had something to do with religion and worshipping. I knew that Muslims and people of the Hebrew faith both believed in praying on the prayer watch which is every 3 hours.

By 7 am the next morning I was up and down stairs for breakfast. Every hotel I stay in I always pay for room and board. Which allows me to receive two meals a day. Breakfast and dinner. Julius and his wife picked me up about 8 o'clock and we headed north to Eldoret East Africa. The scenery was breathtaking. I was in the front seat with Julius and his wife was in the back. Some of the highways was blacktop and in pretty good shape. Unfortunately there is no speed limit in Kenya. You drive as fast as you like. I had to tell him to slow down a couple of times when I saw he was driving over a hundred miles per hour. Every now and then on some of the dirt roads, we traveled on you would see a baboon sitting on the side of the road. I saw someone in a vehicle in front of us throw food out the window to it. As we drove by, it just sit there eating what ever it was that came out of the window. It reminded me of how a seagull hangs around in the parking lot of a fast food place waiting for someone to throw french fries out the window. In the 7 hours it took for us to make it to Eldoret we were stopped 6 times by road blocks operated by soldiers. They had long strips of spikes laid across the highway. Every vehicle had to pull off to the side and be checked out. We arrived at 3 o'clock in Eldoret and went straight to the hotel. The hotel only had two floors and no elevators but it was extremely nice. As we started up the steps, I saw a tall man in a uniform that appeared to be a security guard. He must have been at least six and a half feet tall. He politely said, "Hello Sir, how are you?" I answered him by just saying "Fine thank you, Sir. After getting checked in and taking my bags to my room, we decided to have an early dinner at the hotel. It was already 3:30 pm and I was scheduled to preach at their 7 o'clock service. The hotel had a nice dining room as well as a place outside. We decided to eat outside. In Africa crocodile and ostrich is considered a delicacy and the meat from these two animals are used sometimes. My son Julius knows that I eat kosher. So I let him help me with the menu. As we were waiting for our meal, Julius surprised me with another expense I would be responsible for. Out of the 50 couples coming to the conference, 46 of them were from out of town. He said I needed to give him the money for the place they all will be staying. I had absolutely no idea that I would be paying for all their housing. Right then I knew what the Apostle Paul meant when he spoke of bringing your body under subjection.

1 Corinthians 9:27 because I was feeling my flesh rising up, I did not want to come down on him too harshly, his wife was sitting there with us. In spite of how I felt it was important that I did not insult or disrespect him because it wasn't that bad after all. He told me the cost, it came out to about 6 dollars a day for each couple, which was about two hundred and eighty dollars in American currency. They were all in a 5-story building with forty rooms on each floor. And each floor had bathrooms and showers in the hallways. So basically all they received for 6 dollars was a room and a bed, but everybody

was happy. Before the conference was over one lady came to me and thanked me, she said all the years they been married they never had a vacation. The place where the conference was in a hotel owned and operated by Muslims. The tables and chairs could accommodate 200 people. We started at 9 o'clock every day and I would preach every night. Leading up to the Passover, it was a wonderful week of teaching. It cost a little more than I had expected, but it was well worth it. I learned a long time ago never count up on God. The way the Passover came in 2007 was a blessing for me. The preparation day fell on the seventh day Sabbath. We had services that Friday night and we would have feet washing and communion Saturday afternoon which is the 14th and Sunday would be the first feast day Abib the 15th.

CHAPTER THIRTY-ONE

THE FIRST PASSOVER IN ELDORET EAST AFRICA

When I come back to the hotel Friday night it was rather late. I went to Julius house for a late dinner after church. I had never been there before. So I ask the front desk for a 6:30 wakeup call which I really didn't need. I woke up about 4:45 am and as I laid there on my back thinking about the service I would be conducting. And what made this Passover more different from all the rest, I was doing it on the other side of the world and the people in the service have never heard of feet washing and communion until this week. But what really caused my eyes to start filling up with water was when I began to think about how God protected me even when I wasn't serving him. I thought about how many cars I totaled, and should have died in while using drugs and alcohol. And how many Sunday mornings I would wake up and could not remember driving home, and the three times I was shot at within one month. Those three guys didn't miss because they could not shoot straight. I believe even when I didn't have a God on my side. Even when I wasn't trying to serve him. God has ordained it for me to be here. Now by this time both sides of my face was wet. And my pillow was wet, the harder I tried not to shed tears, the more they came. I rolled out of my bed on my knees and started saying, "Thank you, thank you, thank you" while clapping my hands.

It didn't matter who heard me, I had a need to praise him. I thought about the gospel song, "I am a Living Testimony." When the time came for the feet washing and they had set up everything the way I had instructed them. I had exactly 7 chairs in the front row, seven pans filled with water in front of each chair, and seven towels, one in front of each pan of water. I brought a long towel from home for myself, it's actually four towels sewn together. I also had them to set a large basin on the floor. So when the time came I would pour water into the seven pans symbolizing what Jesus did in John 13:4. So when the devotional service had ended, they turned it over into my hands. When I got up before the people of God, the first thing I did was blow the Shofar. And then offered up prayer and gave thanks to God and the people of God. For about 15 minutes I just did a recap on the Passover teaching we gave this week. Now normally I would wash the feet of the preachers and deacons. And then let the preachers and deacons wash the feet of the rest of the congregation. But this time the Lord led me to do something different, after the scripture John 13:4

was read, I took my robe off and laid it aside. Then I begin to sing the song, "If I wash thee not thou hast no part with me" as seen in John 13:8. And I proceeded to wash the feet of the preachers and the deacons; but this time I instructed all of the pastors to wash the feet of their wives. Now if you know anything about the culture in Africa, men washing their wife feet is simply unheard of in this part of the world.

And you could tell how strange it must have felt to the people by the way the women were smiling and laughing. Once they gotten into it, some of the men started to smile and laugh. I explained to them in the teaching conference it shows humility. When all of the feet washing was completed, I instructed everyone to wash their hands. The communion table was setup to my right. Once everyone's hands were clean, I had someone to read Matthew 26:26. We proceeded to carry out the communion using water and Passover matzah. We had finished everything before sundown and were on our way home. Out of about 50 pastors and leaders only seven elected not to keep the Sabbath and feast days. I was feeling very good about the entire week and I know that God blessed me to be here. It was very humbling to say the least. Everyone came back the next day for the first feast day. Abib the 15th fell on Sunday and we had a glorious time. Just before sundown I was back at the hotel. We had a seven hour drive back to Nairobi the next day. Before going to bed I watched the news on TV. I began to understand a lot of things. Toward the end of 2007, they were expecting trouble throughout Kenya. As I watched the news on TV things started to make sense to me. Why I saw a large presence of soldiers. As we made our way from the airport to the hotel in Nairobi. And all of the roadblocks we encountered. Traveling from Nairobi to Eldoret. I also thought it was kind of strange to have so many security guards in the hotels where I stayed. For example, in Nairobi there was a guard on every floor. And in Eldoret there was the tall polite gentleman that greeted everyone at the front door. After breakfast that Monday morning, I went out into the lobby and set next to a large window overlooking the parking lot and front entrance to the hotel, quite a few people came by to see me off and to thank me for the conference. Bishop Joseph was the first one to come by, he is the pastor that has three sons name Shadrach, Meshach and Abednego. The assistant pastor and the secretary also came by. They really needed to speak to Julius before he took me back to Nairobi. We left Eldoret about 10 o'clock am that morning my flight was to leave at 10 o'clock pm out of Nairobi. We made it to the airport about 6 pm that Monday night, by 6:30 I had made it through customs and the metal detector. I look over to my left and could see Julius and his wife waving at me from outside. They were behind a huge glass wall that was prevented us from hearing each other.

CHAPTER THIRTY-TWO

THINKING ABOUT HOW AWESOME GOD IS

When I made it to my gate at the airport, I had almost 4 hours before boarding. I had plenty of snacks that Julius wife had prepared for me. I had plenty of fruit cake and cookies. Everything is so expensive in the airports no matter what country you may be in. I found myself sitting there observing the people. People that were from all walks of life; I saw people that appear to be from India. I saw people that appear to be from Israel. And some appear to be from China or some other Asian country. And I thought about the one thing we all had in common. We all was created by the same God; and he is watching over each one of us. According to the gospel of proverbs 15:3 and it reads; The eyes of the Lord are in every place, beholding (keeping watch upon) the evil and the good; not only are his eyes on us in this airport. But just imagine how many airports are in this world, and not only is he in the airport he is also with all of our love ones at home waiting for our safe arrival. So no matter where we go the Almighty is there. According to the hundred and thirty ninth division of Psalms, if I make my bed in hell thou art there. When I finally boarded the plane, I had no problem falling to sleep. Every seat had a TV monitor and headset to watch full length movies or television. Coming from Chicago to London and then from London to Nairobi, I must have watched at least three movies. But as I sat on that plane headed back home, all I thought about was how blessed I am. To see people living in such swallow conditions but still have a passion for God and are happy. When I woke up Tuesday morning, I pulled the window cover back. The sun was very bright. We were flying below the clouds. And as I looked down all I could see was ocean. I guess you can say I began to pick up where I left off at last night. I went to sleep thinking about how awesome God is. And I wake up thinking the same thing. As I looked down at that huge ocean, I thought about how many millions of living creatures that God created in this ocean. And if that doesn't convince you he's awesome consider this, this is just one of his oceans. Not to mention all of his rivers, lakes, and swamps and all the creatures in them he created. After about an hour or so, a verse in the bible came to me. It was out of the book of Isaiah chapter 40 verse 25. Which lets you know there's no one like him or can be equal with him. By this time they had begin to serve breakfast. I looked on the TV monitor to see just where we were. The monitor can be used like a navigation screen. We were halfway between Nairobi and London, it will also show you the planes airspeed, how many miles to landing and your ETA. With all of this technology in front of me, I thought about a verse in the book of Daniel 12:4 which says in the last days knowledge shall increase.

CHAPTER THIRTY-THREE

POST-ELECTION VIOLENCE: 10,000 DIED IN KENYA

We landed at London Heathrow Airport on time. I had to change planes in London. There was a two hour layover which really wasn't a whole lot of time. Considering it took an hour and a half to make it through customs. We made it to O'Hare Airport on time strangely enough. I found it more difficult to get back into my own country. After standing in this long line which seemed like forever, I finally get up to this window which is the last checkpoint. After answering a few questions, someone who appeared to be from the security department walks up beside me and said, Mr. Harris will you grab your bags and follow me. He led me into a large room and just said have a seat; he came back in about 15 minutes handed me my passport and said you can come with me. There was about 75 people waiting to get up to the window. But he didn't make me go to the back of the line. He carry me straight to the front of the line. I was able to obtain my luggage in a timely manner. My wife greeted me outside. She had only been waiting for 20 minutes. In spite of the wonderful magnificent trip I just had it felt so good to be home. Normally I am a quiet person when I'm driving, but this particular time I could not keep quiet. Even when I got home it took me two hours to show my wife all the gifts I brought back. I had something for everybody in the church. I had a bunch of pictures and some video tapes. My wife loves to buy pure honey from the health food store. I bought four bottles of honey in Kenya, one was broken in the suitcase. Probably because of the way your bags are throwed around. I was glad they allowed it to go through customs. Things quickly got back to normal. It was time for our National Convocation to be held in Lexington, Kentucky. It was about the middle of the week when I was approached by Bishop Cartwright. He is another son of mine in the gospel. He's a pastor in West Virginia. He also is a professor at the college there. He said, dad I want to give you this young lady's phone number. She's in one of my classes at college. And she is originally from Kenya East Africa. She heard about the work you're doing in Kenya and she wants you to contact her parents. Her father is an overseer with more than two hundred churches under him. As soon as I got back home I contacted her. And she told me she spoke to her father about me. And he wanted me to come to Nairobi East Africa. I was excited about the prospect of going back to Africa that next year which would be 2008. I called Apostle Daily who has lived in Zimbabwe for the last 14 years. But was currently in the US. And he is the director of all Africa Affairs. He felt like it could be a great and wonderful opportunity to bring in more churches. He gave me the phone number and name of a travel agency that no one else could have beat their prices.

Toward the end of 2007, I received a call from my son in Kenya East Africa. I knew the year was almost out because I was preparing to go to the youth council which is always held in December. He was yelling, "Dad I need you to pray for us in Kenya!" I could hear in the background what sounded like gunfire and people screaming as if they were off in a distance. When he finally calmed down enough to make sense of what he was saying; right after the election violence broke out all over Kenya. I knew when I left Kenya that year they were expecting trouble but not at that magnitude. I remember the house that he was in was a rental property. It had a 12 foot wall around it. With two steel doors that meet in the middle when they are closed. He said it look like the entire neighborhood was on fire. The sky was lit up all around his property. He said they had enough food in the house to last about 3 weeks. And he had some board to board up the windows. After encouraging him I told him that we will be praying for his family and all of the saints in Kenya. After talking with him, I told my wife all that was happening over there. And we both went down on our knees and believed God for his divine protection. The violence that broke out after the presidential election in Kenya East Africa in 2007 lasted well into 2008. By the time things began to get back to normal, 10,000 people were killed and 500,000 displaced. The government set up 3 large refugee camps for people whose homes were burnt down. Here in the US there was not a whole lot mentioned on our local news channels about the violence taking place over there. By watching the world news channels we were able to keep up with some of the things happening there. It was hard to imagine this was happening in a place I just left from. I saw one young man being interviewed, he appeared to be in his mid-twenties. He said a large crowd was trying to get into the hotel where his brother worked. And they pleaded with him not to go outside, but because he knew most of them he went outside to reason with them. And he asked them, "Why are you doing this? You all know me and you know that I am a Christian." Just as he said that someone standing in back of him struck him in the back of his head with an axe, killing his brother instantly. I remember when I got back from Africa I told Apostle Daily I believe I have been bitten by the bug. Which is to say I have fallen in love with the country and the people there. So even though I wasn't there it was a difficult time for me. They also showed a burned out church that people ran into for safety, only to have the building set on fire killing everyone in it. One day they showed a news helicopter landing in the open field. There had to be at least two hundred young men and teenagers. The weapon they had were machetes, bow and arrows, pick forks and large sticks. A woman news lady got off of the helicopter with a camera man. After the interview with some of them, she said they were fighting against other people that voted for the opposition. I eventually made contact with the overseers in Nairoba East Africa. I had agreed to be there in April of 2008. Needless to say my wife was a little concerned, but I convinced her that all of the violence was over. I contacted my son Julius so he could make reservations at the hotels. My plane landed Tuesday morning, April 15th 2008. Julius was there to pick me up. He carried me to the same hotel I stayed in last year; Julius said Pastor Hezekiah was coming by the hotel later this evening. After dinner at the hotel I went into the lobby to wait for Pastor Hezekiah. He showed up at exactly 8 o'clock. With him was his wife and two other gentlemen, our meeting lasted about an hour and I was totally surprised at what I learned at this time. I was under the impression they wanted me to run a teaching conference. But on the contrary he was leaning toward becoming a part of the house of God; and he basically wanted to know all about us. I really got excited. My son had to leave that night. He was staying on the other side of Nairobi. He had a long ride back to Eldoret East Africa. The next morning, I mentioned the government head set up 3 refugee camps. But there were still hundreds of people unaccounted for; and many of the children who homes were burned and their parents were either missing or dead, had to fend for themselves. But by the Grace of God, Julius and his wife along with other church members volunteered to start an orphanage. Fortunately I did not need him to act as my interpreter. Bishop Hezekiah and his wife along with the other two gentlemen spoke English fluently. And in that first encounter with him I was amazed to learn that everything we did in our organization they were doing the same thing. The next day he sent a car to pick me up for lunch at his home. It was in that meeting he told me that he would tell me Sunday whether or not they will become a part of The House of God. There were some more officials he had to speak with. Before we had lunch he asked me to pray a prayer of blessings over his home and family. After lunch he wanted me to meet one of his pastors who had a church in Nairobi. We loaded up in his SUV Hezehiah and I where in the back and the two other gentlemen were in the front. It seemed like he never traveled alone. I guess they served as his armour bearers. The church was at the foot of a large hill. It was at this church I would see the type of well that I would be raising money for. The church, the courtyard and all of the property was completely surrounded by a wall with a steel door in the front. The door was not big enough for a car to pass through. They carried me behind this building next to the church. And showed me this well that they installed themselves. They called it a low level well primarily because you only dig down 50 or 60 feet and then they will run plastic tubing down to the water. And run the pump line through the plastic tubing. And if there's no electricity available to run the pump they would use a gas generator to pump the water up. This type of well could only be placed in lowest part of the area. And it only cost about three hundred and fifty dollars American currency. By the Grace of God as soon as I got home that year between 2008 and 2009 we raised enough money to install six wells. Apostle Steven Best in Cleveland, Ohio donated the money for the first well. Apostle Thomas Clark donated the money for the 2nd well. My wife who is co-pastor of the church put on a program and raised enough money for three wells and I donated one myself. We had a wonderful time with Hezekiah and the saints in Nairobi that week. Sunday was to be my last day with them. They sent a car to the hotel that morning. I was to meet up with him for breakfast at the home of one of his elders. We both arrive at the same time. When the gates swing open both cars went in. When we all got out of the cars, the man of the house and his wife was in the yard to greet us. We all left our shoes on the patio outside. And then we proceeded inside before we sat down we all greeted each other. The Elder of the house had family member there we had not met. And then as it is customary I was asked to pray a blessing over their home. They had a long table in the dining room that held about 10 people. When it came time to eat the Elders daughter went to each one of us holding a pan under our hands. While her mother pour water into the pan as we wash our hands. This is a custom. We had a wonderful breakfast. Then Hezekiah asked everyone to leave us alone. Him and his

wife needed a couple more questions answered. After everyone left but him and his wife he began to tell me that they
were married at a very young age. And the Lord showed him
the Sabbath and Fest days. And as a young man God ordained
him to teach and set up churches throughout Kenya. And for
many years this is what he has done. And then he hesitated
for a moment. And looked at me from across the table. And
very slowly said, if I accept the hand of fellowship and we
became a part of The House of God in the U.S., what will
change in the work here in Africa. And I looked at him and his
wife and said, I can assure you nothing will change. The way
God has showed you how to set up this organization throughout Kenya and Sudan or anywhere else in Africa. With pastors in different cities; and you have set up district superintendents to be over certain areas in Africa. The Sabbath school
books you are currently using you will continue to use, if you
desire to look at and use some of our books and reading mate-
rial it would be entirely up to you. God has chosen and hired
you for the work by the Grace of God you have been able to
do and no one can ever change that. Whenever I come to Africa, I represent my church in the US. So regarding this matter,
I believe I can speak for Apostle Embry, Apostle Clock and
Apostle Daily. In regards to your status as founder and overseer you can rest assure nothing will change. He looked at me
with a big smile on his face and said my brother you have
answered all of my questions. Now you can tell Apostle Embry, Apostle Clock and Apostle Daily we are glad to be apart
of The House of God in the US. He also told me that in 2009
he plans to visit the US. His daughter will be graduating from
college and he also has a son who lives in St. Louis. He asked
if I could provide a place for them to stay for about a month. I
told him we would be honored to have him stay for a month
or as long as he needed to stay. And I let him know that the

time he planned on coming there will be a district meeting in Louisville, Kentucky. And I will take him that meeting. To meet with some of the great leaders.

CHAPTER THIRTY-FOUR

MY FIRST VISIT TO THE ORPHANAGE

And then he said let us join the others. As I entered back into the living room the Elder of the house wanted to share a praise report with me. He told me one of the young ladies who was pregnant in the service yesterday gave birth to a young boy early this morning. And she was so impressed with you and what you spoke about that she decided to name her son after you. Well I can't tell you how humbling it was to hear that. Now it was almost 12 o'clock and Julius had just pulled up. Last year it took 7 and half hours to get from Nairobi to his house. But with the new highway it will only take about 4 hours now. But because of all the violence we want to be off the road before sundown. We loaded up and was on our way by 12:30 pm even though the trip was two hours shorter we pretty much went through the same towns. The devastation that I saw in town after town was unbelievable. Before I made it to Africa, I seen on TV the refugee camps the government put up for people that were burned out and became homeless. It never occurred to me that a few weeks later I would pass two of the camps. There was something else that I seen on YouTube before I left the U.S. Someone had video-taped people sitting on blankets on both sides of the road while they were being driven through a town. I never imag-ined that 3 weeks later that I would be videotaping the same events. It must have been hundreds in each town. Eventually the three camps was not large enough to hold 500,000 people that were displaced. We were making good time considering all of the roadblocks we encountered, and we made it to the hotel about 45 minutes before dark. He had me checking in the same hotel I stayed in last year. The same tall gentlemen greeted me as if he remembered me from last year. As soon as I got checked in my room, I went straight to the dining room. The price of my room for that week included free breakfast and dinner. Whether I eat or not it's paid for. After dinner, I retired early because I knew every day was going to be busy. I had taken a shower, gotten dressed and was having break-fast by 8 o'clock. That day I was scheduled to visit the orphan-age. And after that visit, a free clinic run by a man known as Dr. Evans and his wife. Julius was busy and was not supposed to pick me up for another two hours. So I decided to watch television. As I waited for him, and I became glued to the TV. All of these months I was under the impression that the 10,000 people who had been killed and the 500,000 who was burned out of their homes and are now homeless, not to mention the thousands of young men and teenagers roaming all over the country of Kenya killing each other. I thought all of these tragedies were directly related to the election. But on the contrary, the violence may have stemmed from the election but there was a whole lot more going on. In this country there isn't a lot of channels to choose from. And a few that you do have are mostly news channels. There is a group throughout Kenya known as Kenya National Youth Alliance; and referred to as the political wing of the Mungiki sect. On this particular news channel they showed a reporter that was being blindfolded to be taken to a undisclosed hideout to interview a spokesman for the group I just mentioned. I also, learned that the day before my plane landed, the leader of this group was in prison. And his wife was taken out of a chauffeur driven car and killed which set off a lot of violence and looting in Nairobi and the surrounding areas. It was even suggested on one channel by someone who was being interviewed that the young man and teenagers who were killing each other were being paid so many shillings by the government, and not simply because of who you were voting for. It was hard to fathom how much violence had taken place just hours before my plane landed according to the news. The terror began between 4 am and 5 am for residents of Mwiki, Dandora, Kayole, Tasia, Zimmerman. And other cities around Nairobi were awaken to heavy gunfire, eleven people died that day in Nairobi alone. While on this rampage they barricaded roads burnt cars and public transport vehicles. I don't know if I was having a panic attack or not sitting there watching one depressing story after another, I remember putting my hand up and saying Lorde have mercy. I was not feeling depressed it was more like a feeling of mourning a loved one. I had fallen in love with this country and its people. When you think about how many people were killed the last 4 or 5 months, you have to wonder how many of them knew the Lord in the pardon of their sins. The only ones I could think of that might fall in that category are the ones who ran into the church for safety and ended up being burned alive. And the young man who went outside to reason with a mob that killed him with an axe. Death and destruction is literally all around Kenya and it seem like there is no end to it. In the New Living Translation Bible, Proverbs 27:20 says "Just as death and destruction are never satisfied." So human desire is never satisfied. By this time my son was there to pick me up and believe me it could not have been any sooner, I was going through some serious mourning for a country I knew so little about. Finally we were on our way. Even though the orphanage was only 15 minutes away from the hotel, I could still see signs of the devastation that took place in this city. When we came to the front of the orphanage we stop at two large steel doors, which were right in the middle of a steel fence. A very long steel fence I might add, about three quarters the length of a football field. When he blew the horn, someone from the inside open the door and we drove in. As soon as we made it inside the gate I realized that the property was much larger then it appear to be on the outside. I estimated it to be at least five or six acres. Before the post election violence it used to be a market place here. With all types of vendors in each one of the shops. To give you an idea how this place must have looked before it was looted and burned down, imagine yourself standing in a perfect square, and you are facing north looking at a long line of small shops from one end to the other. And all of the shops are painted uniformly yellow and blue. And if you look to the east you will see another long line of shops from end to end painted yellow and blue, but now if you look to the west you will see a long line of cages large and small, which held the livestock.

Such as cows, donkeys, goats, pigs, chickens etc. etc. Let me take a moment to tell you how this marketplace became an orphanage. The violence and rampage that took place in this country left tens of thousands dead, maimed, and scarred for life. Women and teenagers were brutally raped. The parents of many children were killed. And the children had to fend for themselves. Well Julius and his wife came into contact with some of these children. Knowing they could not leave them in the streets to survive on their own, they decided to take them in. Eventually the need for a place of refuge for the children became even greater.. Julius and his wife along with volunteers from the church but most importantly by the Grace of God. When this marketplace became totally empty and available to them they started with 13 children. In about 6 months, they had about 150 children in 2008. I'm almost tempted to tell you how many children will be here when I come back in 2009. But I prefer not to spoil it for you. Instead I'll let you wait until you get to that chapter. My wife and I have a bank in the Chicago, Illinois area where we live. And whenever we have money to send to Kenya, we make the deposit at the bank. My son has a debit card which allows him to receive the money we send. The orphanage is able to operate mostly on the donations it receives. Some of the proceeds from this book will go to the orphanage. But let us get back to the tour, each one of the 30 or so shops that were left were converted into classrooms and office space. Several of them were opened up for living quarters. They had several temporary bathrooms. The first place he took me to was the kitchen. There was no gas or electricity. They cooked on a large cast iron stove. Which was two and a half feet off the ground. Coal and wood went into the bottom. And the top plate has three large holes in it. And three huge stainless steel pots covering the three large holes. Which allowed the heat from the coal and wood to be directly on the three pots. I went to another room to meet the lady who makes all the uniforms. They buy the materials and this lady makes the uniforms. Finally I was being taken into the classroom I was amazed at what I was seeing and hearing. In each one of the classrooms they all had uniforms on. When my son introduced me by saying, "We have a visitor from the U.S., his name is Bishop James Harris. What would you like to say to him?" And simultaneously they all said, "Welcome to our class Bishop James Harris." And then he asked, "How are you today?" And again they all simultaneously answered, "Very fine, thank you Sir." Then he asked which class is this, needless to say they all gave the same answer. You could not help from thinking classroom after classroom you left out feeling like they rehearsed all of the answers. But more importantly these children were sincerely happy. Their demeanor was not that of children whose parents were killed and they have become homeless. It came time for us to leave. We picked up Bishop Joseph on our way to the free clinic. After taking pictures there and speaking to Dr. Evans and his wife it was late and time to leave. I was completely exhausted by Thursday night. I had been on the go all week. But I was scheduled to meet the mayor Friday morning. One of his church members worked at city hall and she made an appointment for me to meet the mayor. We preached at two different churches that weekend. And we left early Sunday morning after breakfast from Julius house. He was dropping me off in Nairobi at Pastor Hezekiah house. And he was going to go right back home. I had a late lunch at Hezekiah's house. My flight was not to leave until 10 o'clock this evening. But he wanted us to stop at someone's house to meet some people that wanted to see me off. The house was on the way to the airport. Once we arrived at the house, I was asked to pray a blessing over the house and all of the people there.

They had a long table in the living room with all kinds of hors d'oeuvres. I didn't have to worry about what to eat, because these were all members of Hezekiah's church. They all believe in eating kosher. Every time another group of people came in they would ask me to pray, people were coming in about every 30 minutes. So I did a lot of praying. It came time to leave so we begin to say goodbye. When we arrived at the airport, Bishop Hezekiah said to me, "Look behind you." And when I turned to look I seen a long line of cars. Hezekiah and I were the first to get out of the car and the cars behind us began to empty out. And it was all of the people that was at the house. Everybody followed us to the airport. And if that wasn't enough, they all seem to want a picture taken with me. I was beginning to feel like a rock star surrounded by groupies. I was the one feeling very grateful to be where I was and rightfully so. But they were demonstrating how glad they were that I was there. After about 35 minutes of taking pictures with everyone outside, we started hugging, shaking hands and saying goodbye to each other. We have made several trips since the 2008 trip. But I really would like to bring this book to a close talking about my last trip in 2011. But before we go there let me take a few minutes to let you know how the Almighty blessed me in addition to going to Kenya. In 2008, the year of my second trip I was made a Bishop. And I believe it was in 2011 I was appointed the state superintendent of Illinois. I received an invitation to go to Ghana in West Africa for a teaching conference. I was not able to make that engagement primarily because of health reasons. It was around that time I suffered two heart attacks in a period of 12 months. We continue to stay in touch with the saints in Kenya by texting or by phone. We were not able to go in 2012 or 2013. And I will always look at missing 2013 as a blessing in disguise because it was September the 21, 2013, that 68 people died at the hands of terrorist when they storm the Westgate Mall in Nairobi East Africa. I have done a lot of shopping there. But I'm looking forward to going back in 2014 Lord willing. But let me get back to my last trip.

CHAPTER THIRTY-FIVE

LAST TRIP TO EAST AFRICA

I received a call about the middle of May 2011 from one of the pastors in the state of Illinois. As the superintendent of Illinois it is my job not only to oversee two state meetings each year. I also support and help them with any problems they may have. She told me she had a problem with an Elder in her church who was ordaining people in her church and giving them license. I informed her that I will be going to Africa for two weeks, and as soon as I get back I will come down to her church and resolve the problem, but the more I thought about it I decided to go that Sabbath. So I called her and told her I'd be there this weekend which was the day before my flight was to leave. And I did go and spoke to the entire church and to the Elder in question and to the ones that he had taken it upon himself to ordain and give licenses to. I had to let everyone know that those license would not be accepted in The House of God. Every license must come through the credential board of The House of God headquarters in Lexington, Kentucky. And we spoke to them about respect for leadership. But no matter what you say to some people they just grossly disregard leadership. I was looking forward to traveling back to Kenya. But I knew long before I was to board that plane this trip was going to be unlike all of the other trips to Kenya that I have taken in the past. Usually the objective was to teach the Sabbath and the Feast days, but this wasn't a teaching mission or to bring churches into The House of God. I was going there specifically to preach and to visit a lot of the homes throughout Kenya and pray for the sick. They had me scheduled to preach in the 14 days that I was to be there in six (6) different churches in different cities throughout Kenya, so I was really looking forward to this trip. And prior to my leaving the week before I had been seeking the Lord and fasting and praying that God would perform miracles. That he would anoint me with a special anointing for the task that I was being asked to undertake. I went expecting God to perform miracles because I prayed and laid out that God would anoint me. That's when I lay hands on people and touched and agreed in his name he would work through us and do the healing, so we went expecting great things from the Lord. Not only did I have the saints here in Illinois praying for that same thing, but we also had people in other states. A good friend of mine I came up with in the church in Norristown, Pennsylvania, Apostle Owens, prayed with me before I left on Friday and I was to leave that Sunday. So again the way was made, the prayers had went up and all that we had to do was make ourselves available for God to us. We arrived at the airport May 29th at 1pm on Sunday. My flight left at 6pm. I think I was through customs and sitting at my gate two hours before the plane was supposed to leave. We went expecting great things. And we were not disappointed, we received many praise reports while in Africa and phone calls since we returned. But not to get ahead of ourselves, let me tell you how the journey began. We landed in Nairobi on Tuesday, May 31 at 6:00 am in the morning 2011. And after making it through customs and getting our visa we started out into the open area where people were waiting for the arrival passengers. After obtaining our bags we began to walk around. And I remembered a couple of years ago I stopped at a service desk and they allowed me to use their telephone. My phone I purchased in Africa some four years ago, was not activated I needed to buy minutes so I could not call overseer Hezekiah from the phone that I normally use in the US and I asked he gentlemen if I could use his phone to call someone to pick me up. And he asked me the name of the person. And I told him I was supposed to meet a pastor named Hezekiah thinking he was going to page him. But strangely enough he knew who I was talking about. He said let me call maybe it's the same Hezekiah that I'm familiar with. He called and I heard him say "Oh you're right here." And he turned to look towards the coffee shop. And Pastor Hezekiah and two of his elders from the church were walking towards us while he was still on the phone. So we greeted each other and began to take the bags out to the car. Because it was very early in the morning and we had a lot to do, he wanted me to get some rest before we started out on the journey that was sent before us. It did not take me long to realize that I was back in Africa because the custom of the people there are so much different than ours. When I said we loaded the bags in the car what I meant was, they loaded the bags in the car. Hezekiah had instructed the other gentlemen to secure my bags and they brought them across the parking lot loaded them up in the back of the van that he was driving. And I was told to sit in the front seat. There's something about the way they treat visitors that you don't get this kind of treatment in the US. I didn't fly straight through from the US to Nairobi. If you ever go there you'll find that you always have to stop either in London or a place called Brussels and change planes or you might even stay on the same plane, but you never fly straight through. I had to stop in Brussels and change planes a couple of times. But because of the long flight and all the time I spent going from Chicago to London, then from London the Nairobi. Pastor Hezekiah suggested that I go home and maybe eat something and lay down and relax because of the jet lag that you experience. So we traveled straight from the airport to his home. And when we got there he blew the horn and someone on the inside opened up the gate. Most of the homes have a large steel gate that is closed at all times. And when the gate opened he pulled the car in. Someone closed the gate behind him and I remember from my past experiences that once you step up on the first landing, you see shoes that are sandals that are lined up outside and I had a pair there. I took my shoes off and slipped into the sandals before going into the house and left my shoes outside on the porch. And the next morning, my shoes had been shined and put back where I had left them. And we went in the house and was greeted by his wife, First Lady Hezekiah. And there was another lady that helps with the housework and with the children. They told me that whenever they go out of the city or even out of the country, they visited and stayed with us for three weeks in the U.S., she will take care of the house. I was greeted by two of his daughters. He also has a daughter and a son that lives in St. Louis back in the United States. The daughter in St. Louis is a nurse. She went to school there and elected to stay. And the son has his own business. He too went to school in the United States and elected to stay. One of the daughters in Africa that I met has been in college for 3 years. The other is in her first year. So after greeting everyone they suggested that if I didn't want something to eat, just lay down and relax. And they would get me up and we would go into Nairobi for dinner. They wanted to take me out for dinner. This is something else that they were accustomed of doing. If we don't eat at the house they take me to some of the finest diners in Nairobi. So I was very tired and went straight to bed and showered when I got up that afternoon because we didn't get in until about 6:30 am Nairobi time. So I was very tired from sitting up on those two long flights. Once I showered and got dressed I went out and had some Kenya tea which consist of tea with milk put in it and brown sugar. That's how most people drink tea over there. There was another pastor there by the name of Peter. He was there for the men's conference. This was the time of the year when Hezekiah has his men's conference. And pastors from all over different parts of Kenya come to participate in this five-day men's conference and because I was a visitor from out of the country, he had his assistant pastor to conduct most of the businesses in the conference, so he could spend time with us and travel with us and do the things that God has called us to do while we were going to be staying with him. He wanted me to close out the men's conference. I believe it was the Monday after Pentecost, but getting back to Pastor Peter he was a pastor that had a church in Edelrid. Edelrid is a town that is about seven hour drive from Nairobi. So we went downtown to a place called the Marble Hotel. And the reason why they called it the Marble Hotel is because they have marble everywhere. Marble steps, marble hallways, marble ceiling, and marble walls. It just looked like one big stone building. It's not that expensive but the food is very good. So this was on Wednesday, the night of June 1st. And on this particular night it was a new moon. He instructed one of his driver to take us home so him and Pastor Peter could go back to the temple and greet some of the other pastors that were coming in for the new moon service and to be with some that had been there all week. So the driver carried myself and lady Hazekiah back to the house. And he remained there. They have a beautiful house with about six guest rooms. And each guest room has its own shower and bathroom with a regular toilet in it. Porcelain is something you don't find too much in Africa. Most of the churches don't have porcelain in their bathrooms. It's nothing more than just going into a small room with a hole in the ground. And that's the way it's done over there in Africa. He told me a few years ago he didn't build the house all at once. He couldn't afford a house like that to go up at one time. He built it over a period of years. And someone in his family went to school for architecture and they helped him to design it. But he's always hosting people from out of town. And other pastors, evangelist and people in his church and sometimes he puts them up. And that's why he wanted a house with at least six guest rooms. Pastor Hezekiah and his family occupy the rooms upstairs and all of his guests utilize the rooms downstairs. He explained to me that he's not a rich man the Lord keeps blessing him. He told me people wonder how he can make it. He does not receive any financial support from the church. He is constantly preaching. He doesn't accept offerings but he said that the Lord provides for him everything he needs. When he has a need for something, somebody will drop him something in the mail and say, "Pastor the Lord laid it on my heart to give you this." And it usually comes from people that are not even in his organization or even in his church. Because the people in his church—although he has some 200 and some people on any given Sabbath—they're not rich people. I would venture to say that 95 percent of the people live in slum areas. If you live in the ghettos, if you're fortunate enough to live in the ghetto in the United States, a ghetto would be considered as second class in Africa because you have not seen poor until you visit a slum area in any part of Africa.

CHAPTER THIRTY-SIX

WENT TO GOD FOR FORGIVENESS

We left Nairobi E. Africa right after lunch on Friday. We were headed northwest, I was scheduled to preach in three different cities Friday evening at the First Church Sabbath afternoon at Bishop Joseph church and finish up at Bishop Julius church in Eldoret. And then fly back to Nairobi Sunday afternoon because Hezekiah wanted me to close out the men's conference. Needless to say it was going to be a very busy weekend. My son Julius was at a funeral; he made it to the church just before lunch time. We were going to be traveling

191

in the van Julius rented. Hezekiah and pastor Peter Maly were traveling with us. We made it to the first church just before sundown. I was told that the pastor would not be there. He had been home for weeks suffering with malaria. My subject for that evening was, "The water has been troubled receive your healing," coming from the book of John chapter 5 verse 4. Before we left I asked to be taken by the pastor's house so I could pray for him. After we had prayer with the pastor at his house, we headed out to my son's house in Eldoret which was a two hour drive. And shortly after leaving, my son said he had a surprise for me. He said remember I told you before you came how the Lord has blessed us with a much larger and nicer house. Well the money you sent for the hotel in Eldoret I used it to buy a new bed and mattress. So whenever you come to visit you can stay with us. I really didn't know what to say. I guess I was tired, but I remembered about something that happened a few years ago at the first teaching conference. I was told at the last minute I would be responsible for the housing for the people from out of town. And I said at that time I didn't like surprises. I guess you could say I am a firm believer that whatever you allocate money to go to it should not be used for anything else. For example, if I send money to Africa to build a well when I come I expect to see a well. But I just told him ok. We finally made it to my son's town. Pastor Peter live in the same town and he asked if I could go by his house and blessed. Now it was already after 12 o'clock am. I felt myself becoming very irritated. I knew that I was not in the right frame of mind or spirit. I think I said something like, "I would love to," but Lord knows I really wasn't feeling it. We arrived at his house about 12:30 am. He called for his wife, his son and daughter to come in where we were. There was no electricity in the house. He lit a candle that was on the table. We began to pray for his home, his family and his ministry. Even though I wasn't in the right frame of mine the Lord blessed us in the prayer. I know what Paul meant when he said "When I would do good evil is present." I thought about how foolish it was of me to be upset because I will not be staying in a hotel for a few days, when this man who is a pastor has been living in these swallow conditions all of his life. But this was not the worst thing I would be guilty of this night. We make it to my sons house about 1:15 in the morning. We were greeted by his wife and children. I could tell my son was feeling pretty good because God has blessed him with a home that he can host his friends, Hezekiah and I both were in guest rooms, and once I seen my room it was rather pleasant. I open the door in the back of the room to find that I had my own shower and restroom, unfortunately there was no porcelain to sit on, but that's okay after five trips to Africa I pretty much have gotten use to it. The room was freshly painted clean and as he said there was a new bed and mattress in it along with a new mosquito net. I really thought I was over the disappointment of not going to the hotel I was so looking forward to, until I gotten undress and started to go to bed. I begin by taking the mosquito net down, if you have never been in a country that recommend using mosquito nets they hang down from the ceiling in the center of the bed. And the bottom part is tied into a large ball about a foot from touching the bed, but when you loosen the ball you can wrap each end of the bed with the net, this will prevent the mosquito from getting into your sleeping area. So just as I began to get into the bed I decided the pillows was the large and went to move one, and under it was the strangest looking bug I ever seen. It was only about the size of a dime. I think I was becoming paranoid. I started looking around the floor, I pulled the bed away from the wall, and seeing another one I looked up where the ceiling and the wall came together and there was another one. And that's when satan really started working on my mind. I can remember saying within myself what the young people would say when somebody has gotten on their last nerve! Or push the wrong button! They would say (oh no he didn't) all I thought about was that nice hotel, the privacy – the wonderful the wonderful dinners – the wonderful continental breakfast – the nice restroom – with the toilet you can sit on, in other words I had gotten spoiled, for a better choice of words I had gotten beside myself. And two things were beginning to happen to me. Number one I had forgotten where I came from, number two I felt myself being lifted up as if I was somebody. In Galatians 6:3 says for if a man think himself to be something when he is nothing he deceiveth himself; but it wasn't so much about what I was thinking that made me know I had to ask God to forgive me; it had more to do with what I almost did. I became so upset I called Bishop Hezekiah on his cell phone. Who was in a guest room down the hall. And when he came I showed him the bug that was under the pillow and I had killed it. His plan was to head back to Nairobi after we leave Bishop Joseph's church. I told him I would be on the bus with him Saturday night going back to Nairobi. Remember I was scheduled to preach Saturday at Bishop Joseph and Sunday I was to preach at my son's church and fly back to Nairobi Sunday evening and Monday morning close out the men's conference for Hezekiah. I was trying to convince myself as well him that this was a good enough reason for me to leave. But he was not buying in to it. He said to me the people have been waiting a long time to see and hear you again, and some have come from far away. It would be a great tragedy and disappointment to many of these people. He said you pray about it and then he went back to his room. I was trying to have a pity party and he wasn't helping, so I decided to call my wife all the way back in the US. I'm

194

sure she'll understand and help to convince me that I'm doing the right thing by leaving. Well to make a long story short I got no help from her either. In fact, what she told me is why I asked God for forgiveness. She said when he first came to this country you provided him with a room and told him when he's able to come back he will have a place to stay. And all he's trying to do is return the favor. And as far as those roaches are concerned that's their culture, you have to remember when this weekend is over, you get to come home where there is no roaches. And the more she talked to me the more condemned I felt about my feelings and what I was thinking. The Almighty reminded me of something that took place 61 years ago when I was 9 years old when I heard my mother cry for the first time. If you cannot remember, read the last page of chapter one of this book again and you'll see that I was almost guilty of the same thing that caused my mother to cry for the first time but the difference is that woman was not confessing to know God. The lesson to take away from this is, Satan is not studdin about you, he don't care how long you been in the church, neither does he care if you confess to be saved, he's going to try to get you out of the will of God. When we finished our conversation, I was grateful and said thank you honey for being open and honest. When we said goodnight to each other I begin to pray for forgiveness. And I'm happy to say that God met me in the prayer. That Sunday morning I went out to breakfast and Julius, his wife and Hezekiah was there we all said good morning and Hezekiah asked me is everything okay and I said yes sir everything is fine. After breakfast we went to Bishop Joseph church, we had a wonderful time there. On our way home we dropped Hezekiah off at the bus stop. Sunday morning we went to Julius church we had a wonderful service there. They brought me straight from the church to the airport. I was back in Nairobi in less than an hour. The next chapter will be a detailed account of my 2011 report.

CHAPTER THIRTY-SEVEN

BISHOP J.E. HARRIS
2011 REPORT FROM KENYA EAST AFRICA

TO APOSTLE GEORGE DAILEY
DIRECTOR OF ALL
AFRICAN AFFAIRS

REPORT FROM KENYA EAST AFRICA

To my brother in the gospel, Apostle George Dailey, we bring you greetings from Kankakee, Illinois. We pray that this report will find you and your family doing well. I apologize for my tardiness in submitting this report. We have had a lot on our plate since returning from Kenya, East Africa, but the Almighty has been with us and blessing us. We arrived in Nairobi, East Africa on May 31st at 6:30 am. Pastor Hezekiah took us to his home where I stayed for that entire week. He insisted on me staying at his home whenever I'm in Nairobi, and because of the long flight he felt that I should stay at the house and just relax that day. He had one of his Pastor's in Nairobi to set up the itinerary for the next two days. Which he had scheduled for me to go out on Wednesday and Thursday throughout Nairobi, praying for the sick and blessing homes of some of the members of his local congregation.

On Wednesday June the 1st, right after breakfast we departed from Pastor Hezekiah's home about 9:00 am Nairobi time. Accompanying me was Pastor Hezekiah, one of his Pastors from Nairobi, and one of his men. We also had a Pastor from Eldoret, East Africa; whose name was Peter Melli. The first home that I was taken to was the home of an eighty-five year old church mother. Who had built this home by herself; the home was built with clay, sticks, plywood, and a few pieces of tin. It had no running water and no electricity; the three rooms were divided by large blankets and the same clay that you walk on outside of the house was on the inside also. But in spite of her living conditions she had the anointing, she had the love, and she had the joy of the Almighty God. She had asked her Pastor to have me to pray for her daughter who was possessed with demons. She also had an eleven year old grandson who had leprosy in both legs; from his knees down to his feet.

The next home that he took me to was a single mother who lived with just her daughter. They lived about 30 minutes from the first home that we visited. We prayed for them and the things that they were asking God to do in their lives. We prayed for the blessings of the Almighty to be upon their home. I have included a picture from left to right of Bishop Harris, the lady next to me is Mother of the house, the lady next to her is her Daughter, and the gentleman next to her is their Pastor. He also is the pastor whose church I preach in on the beginning of the Sabbath every time I come to Nairobi. We spoke of Apostle Dailey about him at the district meeting in Louisville, Kentucky and Apostle Dailey issued him a House of God membership I.D. card.

This is a photo of the Nairobi pastor and some of his members. From left to right you have Pastor Hezekiah, the lady standing next to him is the Lady of the house, the lady next to her is her daughter, the man standing next to the daughter is the father, and again the man standing next to the father is the Nairobi Pastor – who has planned out all of the places that I was to visit the next two days.

We're not going to have enough time to show you all the places we visited. This is actually the last day and the last Family and home the Nairobi pastor wanted me to pray for and bless; which was his house. This took place on Thursday June 2, from right to left is Deacon Willy, I believe this is Pastor Peter standing next to him, and the Lady standing next to him was the Lady of the house, kneeling in front of her is her daughter, standing beside the lady of the house the pastor which is her husband, standing next to him is the pastor's Overseer Pastor Hezekiah, and standing next to Pastor Hezekiah is his wife Lady Hezekiah.

At the end of the second day we went back to the Pastor's church to have a meal. Again this is the pastor who carried us to many of his member's homes to pray for them. In one of the photos you will see Pastor Hezekiah sitting at a table and his head deacon, Deacon Willy sitting next to him; in the other photo there is a picture of myself, Lady Hezekiah, and a lot of the members who prepared the meal that we ate that evening. The church is behind us and we're standing in front of the gate in the front yard. Most churches in Africa are completely sealed off by 10 foot cinder block walls and two large steel doors to drive cars through.

They had an annual men's conference which was being conducted that week and all of next week. On that Friday Pastor Hezekiah had a service which kept him at the church all that night. I was scheduled to preach Sabbath day and with the things that he had to do to prepare for the pastors that were coming from all over Kenya and some parts of Sudan. We decided that it'd be best if I stayed in and prepared myself for the Sabbath day because we had been running non-stop since Wednesday. As usual, I was awakened just before sunrise by the sound of animals, beautiful singing coming from the kitchen, and the smell of good food. Pastor Hezekiah made it in shortly after I had showered and went out to the dining room for breakfast. He was accompanied by two other pastors from out of town. I forgot to mention that my son Julius had made it in on Friday evening from Eldoret. He had planned the agenda for the following week; and he was in Nairobi for a funeral in the day time. I contacted Pastor John Mugo by phone by the request of Apostle Dailey. He lived in a town 5 hours from Nairobi and in order to have him to come we had to wire him enough money to get here and back and spend three days in Nairobi with us. Pastor Hezekiah suggested that I wire just enough money for him to get here and upon his arrival give him what he needed for three days in a hotel and fare to return back home. I preached on that Sabbath day and I was also scheduled to preach on that following Wednesday which was The Day of Pentecost. That Sunday Pastor Hezekiah, his wife, his daughter, and one of his pastors who is in charge of all of the churches on the east coast of Kenya. I have found in the men's conference that overseer Hezekiah's Church is set up almost on the order of House of God-in that he has Pastors that function like our District Superintendents. Following this paragraph, is a picture of us at a fancy diner. Pictured from left to right is Bishop J.E. Harris,

Pastor Hezekiah's District Superintendents, Lady Hezekiah, and her overseer Hezekiah.

On Monday June the 6th I was carried to downtown Nairobi by Pastor Hezekiah, Lady Hezekiah, and the Assistant pastor to Hezekiah. They wanted to take me to a fancy diner in Nairobi for early afternoon dinner. The name of it was Mable Arch Hotel. I'm including a picture of his assistant pastor.

Tuesday the seventh of June, Pastor Hezekiah and his wife left his home very early, he had to drop his wife off in Nairobi. His wife works for a health food store on the eighth floor in a building in downtown Nairobi. He dropped me off at the Marble Hotel where I was supposed to meet Pastor John. Pastor Hezekiah left me at the hotel and went to take care of some of his business. I waited just about 1 hour and Pastor John showed up. I sat and talked with him for about two hours and a half that day. And I was very impressed with our meeting. In his hometown he said that there was at least 50 pastors and leaders that would love to have someone come and teach them about the Sabbath and the Lord's Feast Days. He struck me as a person who was very sincere. He has provided me with some pictures of his church and his family. The photo on this page is a photo of Pastor John and myself.

On the Day of Pentecost I preached in the morning service and I'm enclosing a photo of a family that I received an invitation to come to Holland. To tell you how this invitation came about; there was a caucasian couple that adopted a child from one of the slum areas in Kenya and because of the illness of the child they had to stay in Kenya for 12 months. And in that time one of Hezekiah's members who lived in the same place that the child lived befriended them and became their personal guide. They started attending Hezekiah's church and in those 12 months they've learned about the Sabbath and the Feast Days. And Hezekiah told them about my traveling and teaching. So the fella who adopted the child invited me to come in 2012 to Holland. Hezekiah told me he believes they want to establish a Sabbath keeping church there. I'm enclosing a picture from right to left of the man who extended the invitation, next to him his daughter; who I believe is 4 and a half years old, next to her Pastor Hezekiah, next to him the mother who just adopted the baby from Kenya, and the baby she's holding in her arms is the child they just adopted.

On June 9th we were in Eldoret, East Africa. We left Nairobi at the end of the Pentecost service right after we had dinner, Pastor Hezekiah and myself and my son Julius. We got to Julius's house 1:00 am Thursday morning. Pastor Peter Melli had me to go to several homes and pray for the sick and bless the homes. The last house that he carried me to is a praise report that I will cherish for the rest of my life. There was an elderly man that asked him to have the preacher from the US to pray for him. When I came into the house and met the elderly man Pastor Hezekiah asked him if he wanted him to interpret it for him. And the elderly man said no he could speak English. He said, "I've asked you to come and pray for me because he was being possessed by demons. He said, "A week ago my Daughter left home to go to Nairobi for prayer she was possessed by demons and my grandson went with her to Nairobi and he had leprosy in both legs. When my daughter came home she was in her right mind and no longer possessed, my grandson's legs that were stricken with leprosy are cleared up." Now I want you to understand that I had no idea that when I prayed for that 85 year old mother last week that I would meet up with her daughter and grandson again. But it was on this day that I found out they were visiting from Eldoret. There were many other marvelous works that the Almighty had performed but I just wanted to share just a few of the praise reports that GOD has given us.

On Friday June 10th we left Julius' house headed northwest to a town called Kakamega, Kenya East Africa. I preached for the pastor there that Friday night. The pastor was sick at home with malaria. After the service was over I had them take me to the Pastor's house and we prayed for him believing GOD for the healing. We left that night and went back to Pastor Julius' in Eldoret, East Africa. Early Saturday morning while having breakfast my son Julius came into the dining room and informed us that the pastor we prayed for Friday night who had malaria was up out of his bed walking around and eating food. Which was something he had not been able to do for a long time. To GOD Be The Glory! After we had breakfast, Julius, Pastor Hezekiah, Pastor Peter, and myself loaded up into the car and headed out northeast to Eldoret. I was scheduled to preach  at Bishop Joseph's church that Sabbath day. Bishop Joseph is the Pastor that Apostle Best gave the money to for the first well. On the way back to Julius' house after leaving Bishop Joseph's we dropped Pastor Hezekiah off at the bus stop. He had to get back to Nairobi for his Men's Conference that was still going on. I stayed Saturday night at Julius' house because I was scheduled to preach at Julius' Church that Sunday. He had invited some other pastors to come in. Then I had to catch a plane Sunday afternoon because Hezekiah wanted me to close out his men's conference.

CHAPTER THIRTY-EIGHT

Testimonies

We have come to the end of this book. When I was about three quarters through the book, I came to realize that the Almighty was directing me how to write this book in a way that it will be a book that can motivate, encourage, and empower. As well as holding on and not giving up. But be like Job and wait on your change (Revelation 12:11 says, "We shall overcome by testimonies") so with that in mind I'm going to make the last chapter, a chapter with 7 testimonies in it.

**The first testimony one is by a friend
who is a recording artist
Deacon Eugene Stewart.**

• • •

My testimony, I give honor to the Lord today and to Bishop James Harris for this opportunity to share my testimony with you. It's been 47 years now performing around the world, (20 years professionally), and I've sung with many groups. But one stands out in mind that I learned a great deal from and enjoyed the most. The Mighty Gospel Harmonizers of Lexington, Kentucky was the perfect example when it comes to Business, Budget, Van and Fan Base, as well as connection, they had the perfect package. (Not taking away my feelings for the Morrison Echoes.) Still I experienced deep depression and discouragement, you name it. I didn't feel like I was getting ahead or accomplishing anything. I went to the source that gave me the answers I needed. God has always been that source from the very beginning. My talents come from Him, and with this talent, I wonder why do I feel so discouraged? In the scriptures I came to Psalms 30:5 "For his anger endureth but a moment; in his favor is life: Weeping may endureth for a night, but joy cometh in the morning." Then I continued to search and came to scriptures in the book of Matthew 5:3 "Blessed are the poor in spirit, for theirs is the Kingdom of Heaven." Right at that moment, I began to understand that my whole purpose is to serve God, and make it into the Kingdom. (That's All That Matters). With that in mind, the main scripture that goes with the meaning and purpose of my life. And it comes from Psalm 33:1-3. "Rejoice in the Lord, O ye righteous for praise is comely for the upright. Praise the Lord with Harp; Sing unto him with the psaltery and an instrument of ten strings. Sing unto the Lord a new song; Play skillfully with a loud noise." Since moving back to Chicago from Kentucky, it was very clear in my mind that I was no longer interested in being a part of groups. I just wanted to try out being a solo act for now. But how many can actually say, "God Gave Me What I asked for!" I got down on my knees and talked one on one with God, and asked Him to let me be a example to all who experience the same as I do and to be able to witness and encourage lost souls with the talents given to me. Now remember, I said my desire is to be a solo artist, but I asked the Lord if it be his will for me to be a part of another group, let it be the best named group in the nation. "BE CAREFUL OF WHAT YOU ASKED." The Lord made it possible for me to become a member and favor of The Legendary Soul Stirrers, who was inducted into the Rock N' Roll Hall of Fame. And since I am a current member of this group, I'm the first in the family of the House of God, to be inducted in the Rock N' Roll Hall of Fame. I've been a member now for 10 years; there's been plenty of times being depressed, discouragement, as well as tribulations. But as I learned of them, they learned of me. This is the first time I've had an opportunity to give my testimony. And I truly Thank God for his Love and Mercy, for I put my trust in Him. And I have no doubt in my mind that, "ALL THINGS ARE POSSI-

BLE WITH GOD." Psalm 34:1-3 said it all…the humble shall hear thereof, and be glad…I will bless the LORD at all times; his praise shall continually be in my mouth. My Soul shall make his boast in the LORD; the humble shall hear thereof, and be glad. "O Magnify the LORD with me, and let us exalt his name together. MAY THE GRACE OF OUR LORD AND SAVIOUR JESUS CHRIST BE WITH YOU ALL. AMEN."

The second testimony is from another recording
artist, Delores Washington Green,
and how God keeps his promise.

• • •

I'll start by saying the Lord is my shepherd, I shall not want
Psalm 23. Illnesses can go far beyond doctor visits. It can
become a battle of will and faith. The only thing certain
about life is that it will change. We are forced to keep the
change in our lives whether we want it or not. When I was
a young girl I had a real high voice. Everybody and I mean
everybody just knew I was going to be an opera singer. How-
ever little did I know that God would send me in another direction. That direction would lead me to join one of the most
famous groups in the world. It was the world's famous "Caravans." The Caravans consisted of Albertina Walker, Shirley
Caesar, Inez Andrews, Cassetta George and Eddie Williams.
Much to my dismay I could never imagine this Christian walk
with God would prepare me for what lies ahead. Back in 1975
cancer invaded our lives when my mother and I were diagnosed with it. I never told my mother about my diagnosis.
My mother was a very strong praying woman with cancer
throughout her body. Doctor's was amazed at how she could

still be living with no surgery, no chemotherapy or any radiation. My mother passed away six months after her diagnosis. Nevertheless, I am still here to let you know that God will keep his promises. My next invasion of cancer came again in 2004. I was diagnosed with lung cancer. I had only one (1) surgery without receiving any chemotherapy or radiation and I'm still here to let you know that God is a keeper of his promises. I have lost my mother, father, seven (7) brothers and my own daughter. This is my testimony for 2013 and I would love for you to read your Bible for it is full of healing promises; Psalm 103 verses 2-3, Malachi 4-2, 1 Peter 2 verses 22-24, Isaiah 58-8 and Isaiah 53-5. My testimony is dedicated to all God's children.

I want you to remember this "For without Faith it is impossible to please God."

THE THIRD TESTIMONY IS FROM AN EVANGELIST FROM ONE
OF OUR CHURCHES IN ILLINOIS.
EVANGELIST SHIRLEY L. CARR.

• • •

In the year of 2007, at he close of 7 years of making and sell-ing homemade cookies, it was at that time that I began to notice a change in my energy level. I would get up early to do my baking, but it would take all the energy and some to get me started. I would sit on the side of my bed and would begin to cry, praying and asking the Almighty to give me strength for that day. All of my life I had been a very active person and when it was hard to get started for a days work, I knew there was something wrong. I had stopped selling cookies and had taken a job at a telemarketing suite in Merrillville. I began to notice I was having very sharp pin like pains in my chest and my back, also it became very hard to breathe. I hadn't been on the job long enough to take off, but when it comes to your health, you got to do what you've got to do! June 1, 2007, I called off to see my doctor, knowing within myself there's something wrong in my body! Upon my visit to the doctor office, she advised me to go directly to the hospital to have x-rays done. My transportation was the city bus. As I boarded the bus, I began to get worse by the minute, and as we were beginning to approach the hospital, I started crying because of the pain in my chest and feeling sick. I asked the lady sitting across from me to ask the bus driver to please let me off at the emergency room. He broke the rule and not only stopped but escorted me to the ER door. I had just been there to see a heart specialist and when they contacted him, he ordered for me to be admitted. An angiogram was done. All was well. Then a CT Scan was ordered, to check my chest and upon them doing the test, cancer was found in my kidney and liver. I had very little pain but I was sick and weak. I could barely hold a fork in my hand. I had 22 colonics done from August 2007 to April 2008. I never took the doctor's medicine. To God Be The Glory! I never had radiation, Glory To God!!! And I never had chemo!!! Ain't God good!!! I went back to the Garden of Eden and started taking the herbs that was good for the healing of the nation. I never lost my hair, only lost about 10 pounds and I have gained that and some. Started eating everything as close to organic as possible. Fresh fruits, raw vegetables, drinking distilled water along with fresh made vegetable juice. Refrained from consuming sugars (bacteria feeds off of sugar). No white products, no white milk, cheese, ice cream, fried foods, potatoes. Practically everything I consume was fresh fruits (organic), fresh vegetables (organic). Everything else was green. Why green? Chlorophyll is the most important substance for cancer. And now my oncologist remarks are "YOU ARE A MIRACLE!"

The fourth testimony is one that I heard in Nairobi while sitting in a hotel watching television. A film producer used actors to reenact a supernatural experience, if you ever driven in downtown traffic in Nairobi East Africa, you know there's no speed limit or traffic lights. Well this lady was driving a hatchback and the two children were sitting in the back seat facing the traffic behind her. And the back door flips upward when you open it.

Well the door flew open by itself and the children fell out. When the mother realized it she became hysterical as you can imagine. She pulled over to the side of the road. She got out of the vehicle and started yelling, "Dear God oh my Lord Jesus;" while still calling on the Almighty, she looked up the street and seeing the children running towards her as she knelt down to hug them one of the children said mommy we fell out of the car and a man caught us and placed us on the sidewalk.

FROM THE GHETTOS OF PHILADELPHIA TO THE SLUMS OF KENYA

The fifth testimony is from a young man also from Nairobi East Africa, he said as a child growing up all he ever thought about was going to college, starting his own business and becoming very rich.

Well he grew up, went to college, started a business after he finished college. And became very rich. So rich that when he got up in the morning all he had to worry about was which one of his many thousand dollar suits should he wear or which one of his Rolexes should he put on or which one of his 5 cars should he drive. But as it turned out when he woke up this particular morning, he woke up with a mind to get out of bed but he quickly realized he could not move.

He was paralyzed from his neck down. After spending a small fortune on medical expenses and years of rehab, he's able to get around with a walker. And he's thanking God every day for life. This testimony reminds me of what Jesus said in Matthew 6:33 "But seek ye first the kingdom of God and his righteousness and all these things shall be added unto you."

The sixth testimony shows how God will allow an event to go full circle without any interruption and nothing can stop it if it's in God's plan. If you recall the first time Julius and I met was in the year of 2006 he was invited to preach at a mega church that put him in a hotel for one week, but his visa lasted two months, and God allowed us to meet, and seven years later in 2013 I was nominated to receive an award. There's an organization that gives an award to 20 pastors out of the state of Illinois. There has to be thousands of churches in Illinois. So you can see why I feel honored. But what made it more amazing to me was the place they chose to present the awards. The same church that Julius was invited to 7 years ago. The Lord was encouraging me at a time I needed to be encouraged. He reminded me of the verse in Hebrews 6:10. "God will not forget your labors of love." In that 7 years time a lot of things happened including two heart attacks. But nothing can alter the plan of God.

Testimony number seven is one of Grace and Mercy, in 2013 one of my oldest sons was diagnosed with cancer. We drove down to Pennsylvania. They did not give him much of a chance to live. Both of his lungs had collapsed. The cancer also appeared to be in a couple of places close to his brain. We prayed with him and believe God for healing.

About a week after we got back to Chicago, my daughter called and said he was going home. About 3 months later I had to go to Boston. On my way back to Chicago, I stopped to check on him. His wife and daughter was not home. Just about 4 months later, I got a call from my daughter, he was back in the hospital and they put him in hospice care. The Lord spoke to me and said go back and take your prayer cloth and lay it on him for 7 nights. Now they told me they did not expect him to make it through the weekend. But God said lay it on him for 7 nights. So I drove back to Norristown, PA and I was not able to see him. I don't have enough time to explain why, but I instructed my daughter, my son's wife, as well as the nurses on his floor. The head nurse said she would make sure it would be done. She said we worked with your son at the other hospital. So I went back to Chicago and exactly 7 days later I received a call telling me that my son had passed away. I was grateful to God because the doctors gave him up in 2013. But God allowed him to come home and live on into 2014. And they did not expect him to live through the weekend. God could have taken him on the second or third night but he did not take him until the 7th night.

CPSIA information can be obtained
at www.ICGtesting.com
Printed in the USA
BVHW011714040122
625464BV00002B/72